LAST CHANCE

LAST
CHANCE

∙∙∙

THE POLITICAL THREAT

TO BLACK AMERICA

LEE A. DANIELS

PublicAffairs
New York

PublicAffairs books are available at special discounts for bulk
purchases in the U.S. by corporations, institutions, and other
organizations. For more information, please contact the Special Markets
Department at the Perseus Books Group, 2300 Chestnut Street,
Suite 200, Philadelphia, PA 19103, call (800) 810-4145, ext. 5000,
or e-mail special.markets@perseusbooks.com.

Designed by Trish Wilkinson
Text set in 12 point Adobe Caslon

Library of Congress Cataloging-in-Publication Data

Daniels, Lee A.
    Last chance : the political threat to Black America / Lee A. Daniels.
— 1st ed.
        p. cm.
    Includes bibliographical references and index.
    ISBN 978-1-58648-495-8
    1. African Americans—Politics and government. 2. Presidents—
United States—Election—2008. I. Title.
E185.615.D36 2008
324.089'96073—dc22   2007050752

First Edition

10 9 8 7 6 5 4 3 2 1

CONTENTS

INTRODUCTION

PRESIDENT BARACK OBAMA?

President Hillary Clinton?

At this book's completion in early January 2008, a historic breakthrough in American politics—a black man or a white woman becoming their party's nominee for president of the United States—seems more certain than ever.

But just as evident is the volatility that has coursed through American society since the terrorist attacks of September 11, 2001. One manifestation of that volatility was dramatically displayed this month in the few days that separated the Iowa caucus and the New Hampshire primary—the opening rounds of the final stage of the candidates' march to the party conventions this summer. Barack Obama's narrow victory in the former provoked a frenzy in the nation's media, which declared it was both

Hillary Clinton's Waterloo and virtual proof that white voters had shed any significant racist attitudes, which in the past had limited black candidates' hopes of gaining high elective office. One columnist, expressing the typical view, proclaimed that Obama's victory in Iowa, "a state that's 94 percent white, is perhaps the clearest indication so far that the division Mr. Obama promises to end has largely been put to rest."[1]

Such confidence can surely be described as breathtaking, given that it was based solely on the results of one state's caucus—not even a primary—in which less than 20 percent of that state's registered voters participated, and which Obama "won" with the support of less than 40 percent of those taking part in the Democratic caucus. However, the eagerness of some pundits to pronounce Obama's Iowa caucus vote as the first clear sighting of America's racial Promised Land quickly evaporated when Clinton narrowly outpolled Obama in New Hampshire. The stunning turnaround ignited a scramble among reporters, pundits, and pollsters to explain why their predictions of Clinton's political demise and Obama's presumptive claim to the mantle of Democratic nominee had—at least for the moment—been so wrong. It also underscored once again how critical a role race (and gender) plays within American society in the calculations and contests of who supports whom, who gets what, and why. Much of the media's discussion of the Clinton/Obama results in New Hampshire centered on whether and how race and gender issues (past and present) had influenced the outcome.

Some of the media also noted that the Iowa and New Hampshire results would, in fact, provoke a more intense struggle between Obama and Clinton for the support of black voters. Unfortunately, they cast the contest in the stereotypical and shopworn framework of blacks as a group being "torn" or "split" over supporting one or the other. By doing so, the media continued to miss one of the most compelling "backstories" particular to the 2008 Democratic primary contest and to the 2008 presidential election as a whole: the sophisticated behavior of black voters. Although black individuals have expressed fervent support for both candidates, even a cursory tracking of the polls plumbing black political attitudes since Obama entered the presidential sweepstakes shows that the way blacks as a group have distributed their support between the two Democratic frontrunners has buoyed the fortunes of both. This bundling, in effect, of black support for the top two candidates did not stem from any advice or directive from Black America's political leaders, nor is it just driven by the candidates' personal attraction. Indeed, poll after poll has shown that blacks have consistently given favorable ratings to Obama, Clinton, and John Edwards, but their will-vote-for support, overwhelmingly, has gone only to Clinton or Obama. That is evidence that millions of blacks are pragmatically limiting their choice to only those candidates they feel have the best chance of first winning the party's nomination, and then the presidency. That attitude also heavily accounts for the waxing and waning of black support between Clinton and Obama during the long primary season. In broader terms, this time-honored tradition of how groups, ethnic and otherwise, operate within the American political system is a means of insuring that their vote is sought after—which means increasing the likelihood that the candidates pay heed to their concerns. That the white media by and large continues to be unable to see the old game when it's played by blacks speaks volumes about the misperceptions that continue to drive its coverage of black Americans as a whole.

However, for all that I've just written, and write in the pages ahead about the fascinating contest between two worthy candidates for the Democratic presidential nomination, this book is not only about the 2008 presidential contest. I am concerned about examining a broader canvas: the future of Black America itself.

Black Americans stand at a critical moment. On the one hand, in numerous ways, they've never had it so good: thanks to the civil rights movement, millions of black Americans have been able to pursue their ambitions freely and, in growing numbers, populate the middle and upper reaches of American society. Yet simultaneously, alarming problems continue to bedevil the 25 percent of black Americans who live near or below the poverty line—problems whose persistence undermines the very cohesion of Black America. Black America has long lived with this duality—signs of progress shadowed by constant, marked difficulty. But the contrast between the two realities has become glaring in recent years.

First, the number of blacks making their way into the middle class has raised questions about why a significant percentage continues to be trapped in poverty. Second, the pressures on American society from the economic forces of globalization threaten to permanently chain the disadvantaged to a life of poverty, with disastrous social and economic consequences for the whole society. The high levels of unemployment, frightful rates of incarceration, and epidemic rates of HIV/AIDS among blacks (especially black males) are just three of the warning signs of the implosion that could occur if the crises afflicting the black poor aren't substantially reduced. In addition, the virtual collapse of the Bush presidency and the Republican Party that ushered in the long campaigns for both parties' nominations has propelled the discussion of race matters to the forefront of the nation's political and social agendas. Meanwhile, Black America's national civic leadership is confronting its own crisis, having failed to realize that its very success in helping expand the black middle class required that it turn most of its attention to helping the black poor.

These developments make it all the more important, when considering the present and immediate future of Black America, to remember words written by historian Barbara W. Tuchman. "Leaving things out because they do not fit," she declared in *Practicing History,* her 1981 collection of essays, "is writing fiction, not history." Unfortunately, that observation applies all too well to much of the recent public discourse on the state of Black

America: it has trafficked heavily in "leaving things out," omitting inconvenient truths in order to propagate convenient fictions.

Barack Obama's emergence exposed one of these convenient fictions. The mere speculation that preceded the November 2006 midterm elections concerning the possibility that he might run for president touched off an explosive discussion among blacks and whites—that has yet to abate—about the meaning of black identity today. That frenzy demolished the claim long put forward by conservatives and some centrists that, but for a few civil rights groups, white liberals, and freelance racial activists, Americans have become color-blind and pay no attention to race. By stimulating a new expression of mainstream political activism among black Americans, the Obama-Clinton contest and the broader preparations for the 2008 presidential election have forged a platform of hope for Black America's future.

This does not by any stretch of optimism mean the Promised Land is close at hand. Black Americans must marshal resources from within and without to attack the daunting internal problems they face. These problems will not be solved by self-righteous commands to the poor to "behave" that have been pushed by such commentators as Bill Cosby and Juan Williams. Following the dictates of "personal responsibility" for one's behavior is a code all individuals should live by. But asserting that the problems of the black poor result merely, or even chiefly, from their lack of personal discipline ignores the brutal impact of structural forces that continue to block access for significant numbers of black Americans to the American mainstream. For example, voluminous statistics show that the "prison pipeline" crisis overwhelming the black poor does not result from increased crime committed by blacks. It results from the laws and policies enacted during the "war on crime/war on drugs" years of the 1970s, 1980s, and 1990s—laws that were seemingly race-neutral but whose application has pushed the black incarceration rate to astronomical levels. And while the prisons have filled with black men and women, the penal system has been stripped of job-training and rehabilitation programs. The result: when convicts are subsequently released, they are just as lacking in education and legitimate job skills as when they entered prison. This "formula" for a prison pipeline crisis did not well up from within Black America. It was imposed on Black America. Similarly, the black poor have shown time and again that they know the intrinsic value of work and are willing to take low-wage jobs at the very bottom of the occupational ladder. For the black poor, as for all other Americans, work provides the basis of their identity and influences their sense of connection to and respect for themselves and other individuals. The black poor, just like all poor people, do not need lectures on behavior. Above all, they need jobs that will provide the work and the income to make it possible for them to set foot on the ladder of upward mobility and start climbing. Black America as a whole will need to push to reform laws and government policies that act as structural barriers to black advancement. To do this, they will need the help of the rest of America, of its political class and business class and ordinary citizens. And they must secure that help in the face of several grave threats to America's viability as a whole: the continuing drain on the treasury from the costs of the Iraq war and the global war on terror, the country's looming economic crisis, and the potential crisis over illegal Latino immigration. Most of all, black Americans will have to find a way to rebuild their national civic leadership structure into the vibrant force it once was. The wholesome, necessary development of national black organizations that focus on one specific goal—such as expanding the number of black students in higher education, funneling blacks into the corporate sector, or establishing local black self-help organizations— cannot compensate for the loss of the national clout the NAACP and the Urban League used to possess. Of all the threats facing Black America, their present-day ineffectiveness in promoting government support for antipoverty programs and in devising their own is the greatest. In their example is the most alarming portent for one possible future for Black Americans: their words become faint, their proposals for progress invisible, and they are for all intents and purposes absent from the critical debates of our times, having been turned into relics of a past without a vision for the future. That grim situation cannot be allowed to continue. Fortunately, the 2006 midterm elections and the race for the White House have shown that the ingredients exist both within Black America and the larger society that can be used to forge an alternative, brighter tomorrow. Marshalling the will to do so is Black America's and America's challenge and, hopefully, inspiration.

1

CAN WE TALK?

*America's Proper Obsession
with Race and Color*

On Sunday, March 4, 2007, to commemorate the forty-second anniversary of "Bloody Sunday" and all that the stand at the Edmund Pettus Bridge meant, the two leading contenders for the Democratic presidential nomination—a black man, Illinois senator Barack Obama, and a white woman, New York senator Hillary Rodham Clinton—arrived in Selma, Alabama. Both brought powerful personal and political credentials, and both were attended by a host of supporters, including national and local political officeholders and ordinary people. They were swarmed by the national media, ready to continue its already feverish coverage of the contest between the two.

"We're in the presence today of giants whose shoulders we stand on," Senator Obama said from the pulpit of Brown Chapel A.M.E. Church. "People who battled on behalf not just of African Americans, but on behalf of all Americans who battled for America's soul, that shed blood, that endured taunts and torments."

Just blocks away, at First Baptist Church, Senator Clinton referred to the broader meaning of the Voting Rights Act and the civil rights movement in general. "Today, it is giving Senator Obama the chance to run for president. And by its logic and spirit, it is giving the same chance to Governor Bill Richardson [of New Mexico, whose father was a white American and whose mother was a Mexican national] to run as a Hispanic. And yes, it is giving me that chance."[1]

Representative John Lewis, the black Georgia Democrat who had been at the front of the marchers' line in 1965 and had been badly beaten, put the moment in its proper historical context. "If someone had told me forty-two years ago that two United States senators, leading presidential candidates, and a former president would be walking across the Edmund Pettus Bridge, I would have said that's not possible."[2]

But on that Sunday afternoon, as the celebrants at Selma were basking in the glow of the day's poignant memories and remembering their hopes and present-day achievements, a disquieting dispatch arrived from the Associated Press. Bruce S. Gordon, the president of the National Association for the Advancement of Colored

People, the organization that had done more than any other during the twentieth century to make the civil rights movement possible and successful, had resigned his post because of policy differences with the NAACP board.

Those differences, Gordon tersely told the AP, stemmed from his wanting to have the venerable organization become as devoted to providing social services to blacks as it was in seeking to protect their civil rights. Gordon's resignation, which he had actually tendered to the NAACP board in February, was all the more surprising because he had only held the post for eighteen months. But it seemed to confirm what had been widely rumored—that the former executive for Verizon Corporation with no formal experience in civil rights work had little influence with the organization's unwieldy sixty-four-member board.

Adding to the sense of dissonance, Gordon hadn't gone to Selma at all. The AP reported that he had been in Los Angeles the previous week to take part in the taping of the organization's annual televised Image Awards gala and had stayed on through that Saturday. He had flown directly back home to New York City on Sunday.

Three months later, in the early summer, NAACP officials announced that, to reduce years of accumulating financial deficits, the organization would delay moving its national headquarters from Baltimore to Washington, temporarily close its four regional offices, and dismiss forty people from its national staff, downsizing it from 119 to 70.[3]

The juxtaposition of those two events bluntly symbol-ized the current situation facing Black America. On the one hand, the March 2007 ceremony in Selma was a real-ity scarcely imaginable even in the mid-1960s, when the dismantling of the legal bulwarks of white supremacy generated a tremendous burst of optimism among black Americans. But there they were: a black man and a white woman, both United States senators and the leading con-tenders for the presidential nomination of a major party, journeying to one of the civil rights movement's hallowed battlefields to acknowledge one of its most important anniversaries and to show their commitment to black Americans. The fact that he was a former president of the *Harvard Law Review,* and she was a former First Lady (and graduate of Yale Law School) who represented the continuation of an oft-stated commitment of her hus-band, a former president of the United States, to advanc-ing equal opportunity for blacks seemed to vivify the expansion of tolerance and opportunity in the new multi-cultural America of the twenty-first century.

In bleak contrast, the disclosure of Gordon's break with the NAACP underlined a break with the past in another way. It seemed to confirm what had long been said of the NAACP—that it had calcified. Instead of acknowledging the new racially-tolerant America it had helped bring into being, its leaders were self-indulgently holding on to the romance of the battles of the 1950s and 1960s, while largely ignoring the increasingly desperate predicament of poor black Americans.

The episode seemed to reinforce a growing conviction that the problems besetting black Americans in the twenty-first century were largely self-inflicted and that there was a crisis of leadership in Black America. That charge, long a staple of conservative political discourse, has gained greater credibility in recent years as it has been increasingly adopted by centrists and progressives. Indeed, more and more often, the criticism is made by black Americans. But is it true?

The purpose of this book is to explore the apparent paradoxes of the status of black Americans in America today. That Barack Obama, only the fifth black American to be elected a United States senator, could draw millions of prospective voters and millions of dollars in contributions to his campaign for the Democratic presidential nomination suggests an extraordinary expansiveness and vibrancy within both Black America and the larger society. And yet, black Americans are simultaneously beset by a host of alarming problems that could threaten the survival of Black America as a concept—a precarious status periodically underscored by some outsized event, such as the calamity of Hurricane Katrina. That's how, in the first decade of the twenty-first century, Black America has reached a critical moment. Even as it rightly celebrates the progress made in the forty years since Jim Crow laws ruled the states of the Old Confederacy and a Jim Crow mentality ruled much of the rest of the nation, Black America must see the next few years as its last chance to lead the way in resolving the substantial problems that threaten to overwhelm the roughly one-third of black Americans who live below or just above the nation's poverty line. Those problems include a lack of access to affordable housing; high rates of chronic unemployment and underemployment; poor school performance and high dropout rates; rates of HIV infection and AIDS that approach epidemic levels; an often desperate lack of access to care for physical and mental health problems and concerns; and alarming statistics as victims of crime, perpetrators of crime, and dependents of a criminal justice system they have no choice but to look to for protection. Black America's civil society and the nation at large must remedy these and other deep-rooted social problems quickly. For there is only a moment left before these internal problems become unmanageable and before the tide of changes transforming the society at large—among them, the globalization dynamic and the squeezing of the American working and middle classes; the deepening of income inequality; the polarizing issue of Latino immigration; and the likely calamitous financial costs of the Bush administration's invasion of Iraq—risk overwhelming Black America. Unless the disparate elements of Black America, from its upper class to its poor, can again forge a cohesive national leadership—as it did in the early twentieth century in order to wage a sustained struggle to secure blacks' civil rights—Black America could turn into islands in an archipelago, an atomized collection of social groups whose members feel they have less and less in common with one another and who therefore want less and less to do with one another. In other words, Black America, the entity whose struggle over four centuries for full citizenship defined both the reality and the ideal of freedom and democracy in America, could well cease to exist. The choice is stark and definitive. This is Black America's last chance.

This book was written during the long political season that anticipated the 2008 presidential election, when events such as Obama's entry into the presidential sweepstakes, "shock jock" Don Imus's racist and sexist remarks concerning the Rutgers University women's basketball team, and the so-called Jena Six Case demonstrated anew how provocative racial issues remain. The proof could easily be found in the mainstream media, with its more or less traditional methodical methods of conveying information. But it was even more evident in the unpredictable and unfiltered reaction expressed in the virtual community of the blogosphere. The often-frenzied pitch of the response to these and other events in both media outlets recalls the words that Tom Wicker, a storied *New York Times* reporter and columnist, once used to describe the connection between the media and the American public. In 1983 Wicker wrote an elegy in the *New York Times Magazine* on the twentieth anniversary of the assassination of President John F. Kennedy in which he explored why "the idea of John Fitzgerald Kennedy" continued to exercise "such a lasting grip on the American imagination." Among the many reasons Wicker offered was JFK's sharply honed understanding of the power of television as a medium of communication. Wicker wrote, "During his administration, television—*by now the national nervous system* [emphasis added]—was beginning fully to infuse American life; so television could give Americans the kind of familiarity with Kennedy possible with no president before him."[4]

If Wicker were writing today, he would identify the Internet as the location of America's national nervous system for one reason above all others: it doesn't merely allow responses, it actively encourages them. The dialogue that takes place on the Internet isn't staged in a lecture format, with limited space dedicated to responses as it is in the mainstream media. In many instances, it's typically not even a back-and-forth dialogue but rather a swarming babble of opinion and expression, some banal, some ludicrous, some hateful, some brilliant and insightful. The blogosphere offers an extraordinarily fertile field to sample not only a wide variety of considered opinion but a voluminous mass of unvarnished opinion as well. Both opinion types underscore how obsessed Americans of all kinds are with issues of race and color, how much there remains to talk about, and how often the black American experience of the past and the present is used as the most dramatic framework in which to express those views.

This is not what conservatives and many centrists have been saying for the past quarter century. They have asserted, citing the mainstream media as evidence, that American society as a whole and most Americans have become "color-blind." Their story is that racism has been vanquished as a significant factor in American life, and people today are judged solely on their merit except in those places where the use of affirmative action distorts the process of consideration in favor of black Americans. They insist that it is only the special-interests coalition of the civil rights groups and black politicians and their white liberal allies who have fostered the false notion that race and color is still something that Americans are concerned about.

But the blogosphere has supplied voluminous proof that American society remains profoundly color-conscious and reminded us we should not be surprised. Recall some of the major events that have marked the current decade. It began with the furious protest against George W. Bush's capture of the presidency in 2000, a resistance stoked by allegations of a widespread GOP campaign to deny blacks the right to vote in Florida and other states. That was followed by Bush's appointments of Colin Powell as secretary of state and Condoleezza Rice as national security adviser, setting off wild cheering that these were racial "firsts"— cheering that came from many of the same conservatives and centrists who had hitherto fervently proclaimed their allegiance to color-blindness. However, in June 2003, conservatives were infuriated by the U.S. Supreme Court's

5-to-4 decision narrowing the scope but upholding the validity of affirmative action in the case involving the University of Michigan.

The most revealing moment of that controversy occurred six months before the Court's decision, when both Powell and Rice publicly declared their support for affirmative action after Bush had declared his opposition to it. In doing so, the president's two most visible black appointees joined sixty-five chief executives of Fortune 500 companies, more than two dozen retired military generals and admirals, and the heads of the U.S. service academies who had signed *amici curiae* petitions in the case declaring the country's urgent and ongoing need for affirmative action. The involvement of the companies, which included some of the most prominent in the country, among them, Microsoft, General Electric, and Coca-Cola; and the retired military brass, whose ranks included several former chairmen of the Joint Chiefs of Staff, was the result of university officials' deliberate strategy to emphasize the pragmatic benefits of affirmative action and the support for it among centrist and conservative figures. "Based on decades of experience," the legal brief of the retired military officers began, "amici have concluded that a highly-qualified, racially-diverse officer corps educated and trained to command our nation's racially-diverse enlisted ranks is essential to the military's ability to fulfill its principal mission to provide national security." It later stated, "At present, the military cannot achieve an officer corps that is *both* highly qualified *and* [emphasis in original] racially diverse unless the service academies and the ROTC use limited race-conscious recruiting and admissions policies."[5] Those statements of support stunned the antiaffirmative action forces into a virtual public silence. In writing for the majority, Justice Sandra Day O'Connor quoted at length from the brief and adopted some of its words verbatim as part of the Court's opinion.[6]

The hold that the black American experience has on the American imagination was evident when the gay marriage issue erupted in the spring of 2004 and again when huge demonstrations favoring amnesty for undocumented Latino immigrants erupted in numerous cities in the spring of 2006. Advocates of both causes used the story of the black freedom struggle to bolster their respective positions. They asserted that their claim to be a recognized part of the American nation rested on the unassailable American principles embodied most dramatically in the black freedom struggle.

The conversation about race took a spiteful twist following the racist rant of comedian Michael Richards when he was heckled by two black men during a nightclub performance in Los Angeles in December 2006. And yet that controversy was mere child's play compared to the furious debate provoked by Don Imus's racist and insulting characterization of the Rutgers University women's basketball team, a debate that soon spread to take note of the reactionary misogyny commonplace to both white conservative talk radio and the songs and videos of black gangsta rappers. The obsessive need of Americans to talk about race and color—their perceiving a racial element and a racial interest in nearly everything—even marked the summer 2007 controversies over Major League Baseball player Barry Bonds's surpassing that sport's home-run record and National Football League quarterback Michael Vick's arrest, guilty plea, and sentencing on federal anti-dogfighting charges.

What made the sudden, explosive outpouring of racially driven responses to these events even more startling was that they came on the heels of highly visible political campaigns during the 2006 midterm elections by black Democratic and Republican politicians, which, so the conventional wisdom declared all through that year, "proved" the declining significance of race. Not only did four of the five campaigns involve what would have been racial firsts; each also featured a candidate with considerable personal appeal and for a time each had its own particular excitement. What they also had in common was that all the candidates, Democrat and Republican, downplayed their race when discussing why they were running or why the voters should elect them.

On the Republican side, J. Kenneth Blackwell, the Ohio secretary of state, and Lynn Swann, the former pro football star for the Pittsburgh Steelers, sought the governorships of Ohio and Pennsylvania, respectively. Michael S. Steele, Maryland's lieutenant governor, was campaigning to become the first black Republican elected to the United

States Senate since Edward W. Brooke of Massachusetts broke that twentieth-century color barrier in 1966. Brooke was defeated for a third term in 1978. Since then, only two black Illinois Democrats, Carol Moseley-Braun and Barack Obama, had gained the Senate.

All three, running on the familiar GOP platform of fiscal and social conservatism, had been blessed early in 2006 by President Bush and others in the Republican high command, and, it was said, had the resources of the Karl Rove machine at their disposal. Steele and Blackwell were veteran GOP operatives. Indeed, Blackwell, as Ohio secretary of state, played a highly controversial role in increasing Bush's black vote in his state from single digits in 2000 to 16 percent in 2004, the highest percentage Bush ever received as president from black voters in any state. Blackwell's efforts helped Bush carry the state in 2004, a victory that was crucial to his reelection. If any black politician was owed by the Republican Party, it was Blackwell. Swann was a political first-timer, but the official party line was that his fame and winning personality and solid political convictions would turn him into a credible challenger to the admittedly formidable incumbent Democratic governor, Ed Rendell. In any case, Republican officials insisted that these candidates would show everyone that their party was open to black candidates and could draw a significant number of black votes.

However, in spite of the usual Republican boasts about black electoral breakthroughs, it became apparent by early summer 2006—before the congressional page scandal involving Florida GOP representative Mark Foley sent the party's battered electoral chances into a tailspin—that the campaigns of all three had fallen significantly behind their Democratic opponents. In November, Blackwell would lose by 24 percent, Swann by 21 percent, and Steele by 10 percent.

In contrast, the summer of 2006 was precisely when the campaigns of Democrats DeVal Patrick of Massachusetts and Representative Harold L. Ford Jr. of Tennessee caught fire. And ironically, both candidates had launched their campaigns against perhaps even greater odds than the black Republicans.

DeVal Patrick, a well-connected corporate attorney and former acting head of the Justice Department's Civil Rights Division under President Clinton, was running for governor of Massachusetts. A Harvard College and Harvard Law School graduate, he was well known in elite circles in the state. But this was his first run for elected office, and he was running in one of the whitest states in the nation—one that, moreover, had not elected a Democratic governor in sixteen years. Yet, by the summer, he had shown remarkable savvy and skill in building a statewide grassroots coalition that tapped into voters' hunger for governmental reform and attention to the concerns of ordinary people. That success propelled him first to beat out two experienced and initially better-known white candidates for the Democratic nomination, and then to hold onto a substantial lead in the polls over the white female Republican candidate (who had been the state's lieutenant governor) all the way to the final election. Patrick became the second black American (and Democrat, after Doug Wilder, of Virginia, in 1989) to win a governorship since the end of Reconstruction.

Harold Ford, the scion of a powerful black Democratic family, was seeking to become the first black senator from a Southern state since Reconstruction. He may have been only thirty-six, but he had represented the Memphis district that was his family's political stronghold for a decade. He and Republican Bob Corker, the former mayor of Chattanooga, were vying for the seat vacated by Republican Bill Frist when he retired from the Senate. Initially, Ford was given little chance in the now-solid Republican South. But emphasizing his Tennessee roots and conservative "Blue Dog Democrat" values, he fashioned a masterful campaign that by October 2006 had made the contest a dead heat. In November he lost narrowly—his campaign undermined by the infamous "Playboy ad" the Republican National Committee unleashed against him weeks before the election. The ad, consisting of a montage of images and people meant to mock Ford's various campaign positions, featured a young, blonde white woman who says at first, "I met Harold at a Playboy party," and then reappears to wink and add, conspiratorially, "Harold, call me." The ad proved beyond doubt that race is as vital a dimension of American life, for good and ill, as it ever was. The ad was not conceived by a color-blind strategist, nor was the presumption behind it that the audience in Tennessee was color-blind. The GOP campaign strategy against Ford was, in fact, saturated with considerations of race and color. Yet, all the same, no one could deny that Patrick, in victory, and Ford, in a narrow defeat, had significantly expanded the electoral horizons for black American politicians. Suddenly, it was possible to envision that a host of black politicians would soon be running for highly visible statewide offices. So it wasn't really surprising that reporters and political analysts kept trumpeting them as a "new kind" of black politician.[7] The story line was that these black politicians were "new" and "transracial" because by running for statewide office or for office in white-voter-majority districts, they aimed to attract white votes by downplaying their race and not basing their appeals on racial issues. "Here Comes the New Wave of Barack Obamas," the August 7, 2006, issue of *Time* had confidently predicted in a story that managed to combine ignorance of the country's recent past, condescension, and naiveté. Referring to Ford, Patrick, and Obama, the article ebulliently proclaimed, "Now the next generation of black Democratic pols has arrived, armed with Ivy League degrees, elite jobs at universities and Fortune 500 companies, and political profiles that could make them more electable than their predecessors. And they're determined not to be solely defined by their race."

The analysis seemed to be saying, though it was careful never to put it in so many words, that the "new" black politicians were just like other Americans because they would not be making race a characteristic of their political identity. But *Time* seemed to have forgotten that, in fact, black politicians had been winning the support of whites in pursuit of major offices for more than forty years. Edward W. Brooke had been elected attorney general in Massachusetts in 1958 before winning the U.S. Senate seat opposite Ted Kennedy in 1966. The next year, in what was then a predominantly white Cleveland, a charismatic black city councilman named Carl Stokes had become the first black mayor of a major American city. In the 1980s, Tom Bradley and Harold Washington became the mayors of Los Angeles and Chicago, respectively; Carol Moseley-Braun won a U.S. Senate seat in Illinois; and Doug Wilder became the first black governor of Virginia and the first black governor in the entire country in more than a century. In addition, since the 1980s, numerous black politicians have been elected to secondary statewide offices and the mayoralties of large, medium, and small predominantly white cities across the country. These victories were the result of the winning candidates following the fundamental rule of successful political campaigning—building coalitions out of disparate groups of people. What these black politicians have shared in common was the ability to convince voters not to ignore the fact of their race but to judge them on the strength of their political platforms. *Time*'s coverage unwittingly proved again that Americans are properly obsessed with continuing the nation's long-standing conversation on race.

The black American experience has, in fact, always been the touchstone of society's consideration of what it means to be an American. It was so during the two and a half centuries of Negro slavery and the near-century of Jim Crow American apartheid that followed. At that time, the full purpose of the myriad racist laws, pseudointellectual theories, and theological rationalizations that the white majority in America cooked up about race was not meant just to define blacks and circumscribe their freedom. It was also meant to define *who white Americans were as well*. That use of the black American experience by other Americans to define what it means to be an American continues, mostly but not always, in a far more positive fashion today. A prime motive guiding this book is to make a point that ought to be obvious: Black America is inextricably a part of larger American society, and black Americans as a group are "deliciously mixed up," as Ralph Ellison once put it, with the bloodlines of every group that has trod the continent's soil since the Jamestown colony. Black Americans are Americans. And many Americans who may not know it, or be known for it, are black, as Bliss Broyard explored in the biography of her father, the late *New York Times* cultural critic Anatole Broyard.[8]

Obvious? Not from much of the "traffic" in the blogosphere and in the mainstream media. Some people write and talk as if Black America is, or ought to be, a separate-but-equal world, where the problems have welled up out of something they call "black culture," unaided and unaffected by what's going on in the larger society and, therefore, that can be solved only by black people.

They ignore, for example, how quickly the black unemployment rate dropped at the end of the 1990s, when the economy—for a brief, shining moment—nearly reached a state of full employment. And they pretend not to realize that the words and behavior of the gangsta rappers and the vicious, bigoted language of the loudmouths who inhabit the conservative neighborhoods of the blogosphere and talk radio are two sides of the same coin: both reflect the coarsening of the public culture. Increasingly, many claim they only have black people's interests at heart when they pronounce themselves in favor of "tough love" and declare, "Black people have to solve their own problems themselves," and, "You can't blame white racism for everything." But the economic recession of 2001, which destroyed the economic gains blacks had built up during the 1990s, was not a "black thing." And the cheap Saturday Night Specials and other guns that flood poor black communities are not manufactured in poor black communities. And the record opium crop grown in Afghanistan in 2007, which alarmed drug enforcement officials around the world, was not grown by black farmers and was not shipped out of Afghanistan by black drug lords. And the undocumented immigrants whose presence in America has alarmed so many and raised the specter of a profound polarization of the society are not, by and large, of African descent. None of these transformations is narrowly the fault or consequence of the black community however you define it.

Furthermore, it is irresponsible to pretend that Black America is unaffected by such broader forces as the transformation of the American workplace; the interplay of the country's multiracial, multiethnic, and multicultural groups; the ramifications of illegal Latino immigration; and the potentially catastrophic consequences of the Bush administration's foreign policy blundering in confronting global terrorism and mismanagement of such domestic responsibilities as the budget and the federal disaster relief program. The reach of global capitalism and the revolution in communications technology to every corner of the world has meant that very few Americans of whatever ethnic, racial, and economic background live segregated lives anymore. Almost all of us interact with individuals and groups of people who are different from us in important respects. For that reason alone, it is a significant denial of reality to discuss race and color in America as if it were, first, literally *just* a matter of black and white; and second, *only* a matter of race and color.

Black America's fortunes have always been directly linked to and dependent upon those of the larger society, just as America's good fortune owes a great deal to the contributions of black Americans. One piece of irrefutable proof is grounded in that most venerated achievement of

Black America: the civil rights movement of the mid-twentieth century. It's not fashionable to say so, but the movement owed its success to white people.

This isn't to validate the assertion some have made that at a crucial moment, Everett Dirksen, the crusty Republican senator from Illinois, "gave" America the landmark Civil Rights Act of 1964 and the Voting Rights Act of 1965. Even more laughable is the claim that Paul "Bear" Bryant, the legendary football coach of the University of Alabama, "did more for civil rights" in the South than Martin Luther King Jr. by finally integrating his football team in 1970. Nothing can diminish the extraordinarily shrewd and brave and determined effort that Black America mounted in the aftermath of the 1896 U.S. Supreme Court decision in *Plessy v. Ferguson.*

That decision upheld a Louisiana law that segregated blacks and whites on railroads and other forms of public transit. The decision asserted the preposterous claim that segregation was not unjust as long as the white-run state and local governments provided facilities for blacks that, though separate, were equal to those whites enjoyed. *Plessy* put the Court's moral weight behind the burgeoning racist laws in the South and customs in the North that were confining blacks to an ever-smaller corner of American life at the turn of the century. *Plessy* buried the promise implicit in blacks' emancipation from slavery after the Civil War and returned them to the stateless status they were assigned in 1857 by the Supreme Court ruling on *Dred Scott v. Sanford.*

Dred Scott had been enslaved in Missouri. When his owner, a military officer, was assigned posts in the free states of Wisconsin and Illinois, he took Scott with him and spent several years in each state. When they returned to Missouri, Scott sued for his freedom, asserting that living in free territories had made him free. Lower courts ruled in Scott's favor. But when the case reached the Supreme Court, its majority declared that Scott was not a free man. Chief Justice Roger B. Taney, a staunch supporter of Negro slavery, went further. He asserted that no black Americans—even the so-called free blacks, those not held in bondage (about 500,000 of the 4 million blacks in the United States in the 1850s)—had ever been or could ever be citizens of the United States. Therefore, Taney proclaimed, Dred Scott had no right to sue because, being black, he "had no rights which the white man was bound to respect." The Taney Court's decision, which also declared that slavery could not be barred from any of the country's states or territories, made the Civil War a certainty.[9]

In *Plessy*'s wake, black Americans set out to save themselves and to, as the poet Langston Hughes would write, "make America be America." White Americans did not "give" black Americans their rights. It was Black America that taught White America what democracy means.

But it's equally undeniable that blacks' twentieth-century civil rights movement would have failed—just as Black America's effort to grasp the rights of citizenship during the Reconstruction era failed—were it not for the accommodation made by a crucial sector of White Amer-

ica. A critical minority of white American institutions—
the courts, foundations, colleges and universities, labor
unions, major corporations and small businesses, and the
federal government and local and state governments outside the South—made the widespread adoption of the
civil rights movement's agenda possible.

The history of the 1950s and 1960s thus provided an
ironic reversal of the nineteenth-century triumph of white
supremacy over Reconstruction. In 1895, the year before
the *Plessy* decision, Booker T. Washington delivered his
famous "Five Fingers Speech" at the Atlanta Exposition,
pledging the surrender of blacks' quest for civil rights and
their *accommodation* to the brutal white racism of the time.
Much of White America rejoiced, and the following year
Harvard University awarded Washington an honorary
master's degree. But throughout the twentieth century, it
was White America that did the racial accommodating
as Black America kept pushing to move forward. The accommodation was often slow and grudging; it took sev-
enty years, after all. But it did happen. It began in earnest
in the early 1900s, as whites (along with black church
denominations) played significant roles in the founding
and funding of numerous Negro colleges and in the National Urban League (1909) and NAACP (1910). It was
reflected, too, in the unceasing demand of the growing
industrial centers of the North for skilled and unskilled
laborers of all kinds to propel the country's growing economic might. That opportunity, limited though it was by
Northern whites' considerable bigotry, nonetheless was

the "pull" that complemented the incentive to migrate that ultimately millions of Southern blacks would feel from the even greater brutality of legalized racism. In the century's middle decades, through the presidencies of Franklin Delano Roosevelt, Harry S. Truman, Dwight D. Eisenhower, John F. Kennedy, Lyndon Baines Johnson, and, yes, Richard Nixon, a crucial segment of America's national white leadership in politics, the courts, labor, higher education, business, religion, and philanthropy worked assiduously to modernize America's racial posture. Whatever their personal feelings about blacks, all understood that those decades' principal moral challenges—the Great Depression; World War II's fight against the brutal doctrines and the pursuit of conquest of Japan and Germany; the "bitter peace" of the cold war against the Soviet Union; and the independence movements of the 1950s and 1960s against European colonialism—made it imperative that the United States shed not only its system of *de jure* apartheid but also the more overt facets of *de facto* apartheid. That accommodationist force within white leadership is even more institutionalized today—as the coalition that united to support affirmative action in the University of Michigan case before the Supreme Court showed. Black America and White America are America.

Of course, not everyone agreed. One aspect of the white conservative reaction to the push of blacks for full citizenship during the 1960s, termed "white backlash," was the

implicit and explicit attempt to divide the histories of
white and black Americans. That conservative stance has
been even more pronounced since the first Reagan election, though that doesn't necessarily imply greater popularity. It has, though, had an effect on the ability of liberal
and centrist white political leadership to continue to ac-
commodate blacks' demands for systemic advancement
because it has seemed, falsely, to separate the agendas of
the black and white middle classes. The last quarter century of national politics has seen a narrowing of affirmative
action policies, greater segregation of the nation's public
schools, and the continuing pervasive residential segregation of American neighborhoods. This is evidence, on the
one hand, of political progressives' failure of nerve, and, on
the other, of America continuing to grapple with issues
that were topics of debate during the civil rights years.

The hostility of the administrations of Ronald Reagan
and George H. W. Bush to the interests of the black
masses, not just a clutch of black progressive organizations,
is well documented. So, too, is the "fifth-column" work
that George W. Bush's administration has employed, using
its political-appointment power to subvert the mandates of
the Equal Employment Opportunity Commission and the
Civil Rights Division of the Justice Department, to name
just two federal agencies, to protect the rights of black
Americans.

The current Bush administration's deliberate attempt to
violate federal rules protecting blacks' rights demands that
we ask some uncomfortable questions about the quality of

the national white political leadership of our era. The decline in the quality of America's national political leadership—for which the Democratic Party must also share some blame—has been chronicled in a host of books, such as Thomas Mann's and Norman Ornstein's scathing critique of the Congress and the posture of the Bush administration toward Congress in *The Broken Branch: How Congress is Failing America and How to Get It Back on Track*. Mann and Ornstein are careful to point out that Congress's decline as a deliberative body is not simply a matter of having "bad" people there, but the result of specific systemic forces that originated from both within and without Congress and the national political structure.

The decline of Congress and the diminished performance of a significant segment of America's white leadership, undermined by negative systemic forces, have made it inevitable that part of America's black leadership would also be affected. There is a link between the failure of politically progressive leadership in Congress and other areas of government and the lack of vision and vigor the NAACP and, to a lesser extent, the National Urban League have shown since the early 1990s. What happens to part of America can happen to all of America. True, those organizations faced a very challenging environment: conservatism has dominated the political agenda since the 1980s, and there has seemed to be little concern among elected officeholders or the mainstream media about exploring progressive proposals for advancing blacks' interests. But finding a way out of that cul-de-sac requires leadership, and, while numerous local chapters of the NAACP and Urban League have made valuable contributions to their communities, by and large the national leadership of Black America's two most important national organizations failed.

Their decline in influence and achievement was partly offset by the emergence of a constellation of function-specific groups. As the description implies, they are not umbrella organizations (like the NAACP and the Urban League); instead they limit themselves for the most part to a few specific purposes. Some are national organizations, such as the National Black MBA Association, whose membership is comprised of black business school alumni and students; or the Jackie Robinson Foundation, which provides scholarships for undergraduate and graduate students and summer internships with various businesses. Some confine their work to particular local areas, such as the Partnership of Boston, which works with middle managers and executives of color at Boston-area corporations to advance the interests of diversity. Others define their mission even more narrowly. Hale House Center in Harlem, New York, provides shelter to infants abandoned or given up by their parents as well as to young mothers of infants; and Harlem's Children's Zone operates as a comprehensive social service organization helping the neighborhood's at-risk children and adolescents.

All of these groups, and many more, including black individuals and black caucuses inside white institutions ranging from law firms and corporations to universities and foundations, are doing work that, overwhelmingly, used to be virtually the exclusive province of the NAACP and the National Urban League. Their focus is sharp and specific, but it is also limited. In almost all cases, it feels "local" rather than nationally ambitious. So despite the welcome expansion of organizations pressing the advancement of black Americans in particular occupational and social niches, there remains a pressing need for the kind of national campaign leadership that the NAACP and National Urban League used to provide—that once had the clout to press the point that American and black American be seen as absolutely complementary and overlapping.

There is, in addition, another group of black leaders—who have largely escaped public scrutiny for a quarter century—that must also be called to account: black conservatives. Neither of black conservatism's two wings—its intellectual advocates, such as Shelby Steele, Thomas Sowell, and John McWhorter, nor its political operatives, such as J. Kenneth Blackwell and Michael S. Steele—has succeeded in making it a viable political option for any sizable segment of black Americans. On the contrary, black Republicans have compiled an astonishing record of electoral failure over the past two decades. For example, of the sixty-four black Republicans who ran for Congress in the four national elections from 1998 to 2004, a span that marked the zenith of the GOP's political power, all but one lost (the exception was former Rep. J. C. Watts of Oklahoma, who first won election in 1994 and left Congress in 2002); and fifty-two of them lost by more than twenty-five percentage points.[10]

This sorry electoral history and lack of any discernible policy influence in an era when the GOP and political conservatism have been so dominant raises a host of questions about the motives of the GOP high command and their black conservative fellow travelers. Their performance during a period that witnessed the explosive growth of a new black middle class—a class that among other ethnic groups has always been highly susceptible to conservative political appeals—represents a profound failure of the responsibility to Black America they have long claimed to be exercising. Since the beginning of the Reagan administration, black Republicans declared they had the necessary ideas and contacts with those in power to reduce the problems bedeviling Black America. But they have produced no legislation or bureaucratic policies of any substance. Indeed, except for Supreme Court Justice Clarence Thomas, black conservatives have yet to produce any individual national political figure of note. Much as it's important to challenge black progressive leadership for its ineffectiveness during an era of conservative dominance, it's also essential to mark the record of black conservatives as far worse. For that failure has contributed significantly to the ongoing predicament black Americans have faced in American politics. That is, that unlike all other American ethnic groups, their support has been sought by only one major political party at a time. One need not dig too deeply to realize that, contrary to the numbingly conventional wisdom, it's not the Democratic Party but the Republican Party that has taken Black America for granted, and black conservatives have been aiders or abetters. It is hard to overstate the harm caused by this structural barrier—blacks being limited to one-party politics—to a fully evolved black politics. It profoundly limits blacks' chances to gain a full measure of benefits from America's political system.

2

NEVER HAD IT
SO GOOD . . . BUT

It was just a "dress" picture on the front page of the *New York Times* business section, one done merely to provide what journalists call visual texture to a long profile of Bruce Wasserstein, the well-known chairman of the investment bank of Lazard ("The Adviser Who Became the Activist," February 26, 2006). The picture, which showed Wasserstein and two of his colleagues in a moment of informal discussion, didn't really have anything to do with the thrust of the profile. Neither the point of the picture nor of the story itself was to show that the two men with Wasserstein at the top of one of the world's storied investment firms were black Americans.

That's precisely why, in one sense, the photo of Bruce Wasserstein discussing business with William M. Lewis Jr.

and Vernon Jordan, the former civil rights leader and "First Friend" of former president Bill Clinton, quietly spoke volumes about the advances black Americans have made in American society.

Since the early 1990s, there has been an unmistakable speeding up of the inclusion of blacks at the highest levels of American society that would have surprised even the sunniest optimist in the 1960s. Black Americans have never been so well situated in America; they've never had it so good.

Black Americans now occupy senior posts at major print and electronic media outlets. They're a highly visible presence on the faculties and in the student populations of the nation's elite colleges, and, now, in the office of the president at major universities. Their numbers in the corporate suites remain small, but a few have risen to head some of the most visible Fortune 100 companies. The world's greatest golfer, Tiger Woods, whom Americans name as their favorite sports star, is the brown-skinned son of a black American husband and his Thai-born wife. America's favorite female athlete, Serena Williams, one of the world's top tennis stars, is a black woman whose parents honed her talents on the public tennis courts of predominantly black Compton, California. Venus Williams, Serena's sister and also a top tennis star, is America's third-favorite female athlete. Oprah Winfrey, America's favorite television personality for the last five consecutive years, wields a cultural clout few in American history, male or female, have ever surpassed—or even equaled. The sense that blacks were making breakthroughs in many areas of society seemed particularly clear when audiences, watching the collegiate national championship of the 2007 football season, saw both contesting teams, Ohio State University and the University of Florida, being led by their star players—black quarterbacks. Several weeks later, on one day over one weekend in pro football, the Indianapolis Colts beat the New England Patriots to gain a berth in the Super Bowl, making their widely respected head coach, Tony Dungy, the first black man to coach a team all the way to that iconic event. A few hours later, when the Chicago Bears beat the New Orleans Saints to gain the Super Bowl's other berth, the Bears' coach, the widely respected Lovie Smith, became the second black coach to have that honor.

Perhaps most spectacularly, blacks seem better woven into the political fabric of the nation than ever before. After all, the last two presidents of the United States—one Democratic, one Republican—have appointed black Americans to important cabinet posts, and three of those individuals were close personal friends of the president. President Clinton appointed blacks to several cabinet-level positions—heads of the departments of Veteran Affairs, Agriculture, Labor, and Commerce; he also appointed a black to serve as surgeon general. Alexis Herman and Ronald H. Brown, appointed to head the departments of Labor and Commerce, respectively, were personal friends as well as experienced political operatives who helped engineer Clinton's rise from governor of Arkansas to the White House. In addition, Clinton named blacks to several powerful subcabinet posts, including director of the Office of Management and Budget and the chair of the Federal Communications Commission. All of those appointments marked the first time blacks had held such positions. During his first administration, President George W. Bush continued the momentum of black cabinet-level racial breakthroughs by appointing Colin Powell as secretary of state and naming Condoleezza Rice, one of his inner circle of longtime political advisers, to the White House post of national security adviser. Rice, of course, subsequently became secretary of state during Bush's second term. Bush also appointed a black man (Rod Paige) to the post of secretary of Education during his first term and another (Alphonso Jackson) to serve as secretary of Housing and Urban Development during his second term; and he named Lurita Alexis Doan, a private entrepreneur, to head the General Services Administration, and Claude Allen, a black conservative operative, to be White House domestic policy adviser. The Democratic Party's capture of Congress in November 2006 elevated four black Democrats to major committee chairmanships and another dozen or so to significant subcommittee chairmanships.

Equally important, the markers that substantial numbers of blacks are now ensconced in the American middle class are unmistakable. For example, more than 50 percent of blacks who are employed work in white-collar jobs, and more than 25 percent hold managerial positions.[1] Nearly half, 48 percent, of black Americans owned their homes in 2005.[2] More than 50 percent of blacks have middle-class incomes.[3] And black enrollments in all sectors of higher education, from community colleges to graduate and professional schools, have continued to increase. The 2.1 million blacks in higher education constitute 11.7 percent of the roughly 18 million students enrolled, a number nearly equal to their proportion of the college-age population of society as a whole.[4] All this would seem to suggest that the problems of Black America are history, perhaps even that Black America makes the greatest progress when it comes to think of itself as a minority with a unique social and political agenda.

But in fact, it's clear that America's racial Promised Land is still far off in the distance. The growth of the black middle class and the attention-grabbing breakthroughs resonate so vividly because they testify to the great expansion of opportunity for blacks since the 1960s. But at the same time, the grave problems looming over Black America continue to cloud the horizon, leaving many in desperate straits. The two conditions—dramatic achievement for some; desperation for others—coexist within Black America to a striking degree. Indeed, even the breakthroughs themselves can obscure how inconsequential the progress has actually been.

In collegiate and pro football, blacks have long played starring roles at every position, and they make up more than 40 percent of the players in both. But as head coaches, who are overwhelmingly drawn from the ranks of former players, the scarcity of blacks is startling. Only six blacks have served as head coach of a team in the thirty-two team National Football League over the course of its seventy-odd-year history, and three of those men were appointed in the last five years. The place of black and Hispanic coaches in the even clubbier world of college football is worse. Just seven of the 119 colleges and universities in the National Collegiate Athletic Association's top division—where the football powerhouses from the University of Southern California to Florida play—are black or Hispanic. (The high-water mark for one year was eight in 1998.) Two of those coaches were hired after the 2006 collegiate season—when there were a total of twenty vacancies open.[5]

The continued exclusion of blacks and Hispanics from all but a token number of the top jobs in football and other sports stems from the same forces limiting their representation in most other well-salaried professions: money and influence. A growing number of head coaching positions offer lucrative contracts, which often contain clauses providing other opportunities to make even more money. Coaches of the top college teams sit at the center of a multimillion-dollar industry involving alumni and local and national businesses and corporations of vital importance to the college or university's financial well-being.

The scarcity of blacks in high and high-salaried positions of power and influence in collegiate and professional football carries over to institutions of higher education. Despite the picture portraying the nation's predominantly white colleges and universities as havens of "diversity" peopled by large numbers of black Americans, the reality is significantly different. According to surveys conducted by the *Journal of Blacks in Higher Education (JBHE)*, only 5.2 percent of all full-time faculty members are black, a figure that has increased just 1 percentage point in 2 decades. That figure is somewhat misleading, however, because the percentages of black full-time faculty at all but 5 of the 28 highest-ranked universities are markedly less. At Atlanta's Emory University, 6.8 percent of its 2,710 full-time faculty are black, and the figures at Columbia University, the University of North Carolina at Chapel Hill, the University of Michigan, and Brown University are also at or above the national average. The rest, including such institutions as Vanderbilt, Northwestern, Yale, Rice, Wake Forest, Carnegie Mellon, Princeton, and the University of Virginia, are below—often substantially below—the national average. Harvard's black faculty and the work of its Afro-American Studies Department have garnered much attention since the early 1990s, but as of 2005, only 93, or 3.1 percent, of the university's 2,959 full-time faculty were black.

The situation at twenty-five of the most prominent liberal arts colleges, whose faculty numbers ranged from 85 to 347, is little better. The same 2007 *JBHE* survey found that seven met the national average of 5.2 percent; the rest did not. Finally, of the country's fifty flagship state universities, only five—the universities of North Carolina at Chapel

Hill, Georgia, Michigan, Maryland, and Mississippi—were at or above the national average. Typically, such low numbers are excused by pointing to the relatively small numbers of blacks pursuing doctorates. But the *JBHE* editors said that the level of black faculty at an institution most often depends on whether its faculty has "a strong commitment to developing a racially-diverse teaching corps" and whether the power to hire faculty rests primarily with the individual academic departments or with the institution's deans and other top officials. They commented: "The 'no blacks in the PhD pipeline' thesis is at worst a red herring and at best a weak explanation for poor results." The *JBHE* soberly concluded that, at the current rate of progress, it will take another 192 years for the percentage of black full-time faculty in higher education to reach 12 percent—black Americans' current percentage of the American population.

This same glacial pace characterizes the rate at which blacks are achieving partnerships in major American law firms. In 2000, there were 1,608 black, Hispanic, and Asian-American partners in the nation's major law firms, about 3.4 percent of the total. By 2005 that figure had increased to 4 percent of the total, or nearly 2,200 of the nation's 54,000 law firm partners. Fifteen percent of these firms' 61,000 associates were people of color. Theodore V. Wells Jr., a partner at Paul, Weiss, Rifkind, Wharton & Garrison in New York and one of the nation's top trial lawyers, told the *New York Times* that the source of the problem lay in "a continuing revolving door [cycle], where

a fairly constant number of minority associates comes into
the pipeline, and they're gone four years later, with the net
result being a continually small number of minority senior
associates and an even smaller number of minority partners. . . . It's taken us almost fifteen years to get to the
point where most large firms now have one African American partner."[6]

The gap that exists between the highly visible and celebrated black achievements and the more common and often more troubling everyday reality was underscored by
the agreement carved out in the fall of 2006 between advertising firms based in New York City—the hub of the
worldwide advertising industry—and the city's Human
Rights Commission. Prompted by complaints of discrimination from several black workers, the city agency had
launched an investigation that produced startling results:
it found the industry's record on hiring and promoting
people of color to senior positions had barely changed in
forty years. The city commission's examination of sixteen
of the largest ad agencies—including such powerful companies as Saatchi & Saatchi, Ogilvy & Mather, and
DDB—found that few agencies employed blacks in their
senior and creative positions. Patricia Gatling, the chair
of the commission, told a special panel discussion convened in Washington in September 2006 by the Congressional Black Caucus that one ad agency "went so far as to
identify the African American chief of security and director of janitorial services as company managers."

As one would expect, the lack of blacks at the companies' senior levels meant that few blacks earned high salaries. Twenty-two percent of the companies' 8,000 employees earned annual salaries in excess of $100,000, but just 2.5 percent of these employees were black. At DDB's New York office, for example, 59 of the 476 employees were black. But of the 159 employees who earned salaries of $100,000 or more, only 2 were black. Neither of them was among the 29 agency employees who earned from $200,000 to $300,000 a year, or the 22 who earned more than $300,000 annually. Other ad agencies had worse records. "In a city where African Americans make up one quarter of the population, with billions of dollars in purchase power, the lack of representation in the advertising industry is completely unacceptable," Gatling told the CBC panel. "There are plenty of [black] secretaries and clerks, but very few African Americans have risen much higher."

In other words, the nation's advertising industry bolstered its clients' needs to appeal to the nation's increasingly diverse population by producing ads displaying an idealized, integrated society. But the agencies themselves were resolutely clinging to past practices. In 1968 and 1978, the predecessor agencies to the New York's Human Rights Commission had issued reports calling on the advertising industry to improve its hiring and promotion practices. Nothing had happened. This time, the commission forced the companies to sign written agreements that

set numerical goals for hiring and promotion to managerial positions and it required annual progress reports until
2009. The companies also agreed to establish recruiting
and internship programs through colleges and universities
with large minority student populations and to link their
managers' compensation to the goals of the agreement.

Perhaps the starkest demonstration of the continuing
tension between progress and stagnation when it comes
to expanding opportunity across the color line can be seen
in an arena many might at first glance consider frivolous:
the fashion industry. In the fall of 2007, both the *Washington Post* and the *New York Times* wrote lengthy articles
about the growing scarcity of black models in the fashion
shows that leading designers regularly stage to promote
their collections in Europe and America. Where once
black models were ubiquitous on the runways of the most
prestigious shows and in the pages of the most prominent
fashion magazines, now, the articles reported, they have
all but disappeared. The *Times* article noted that of the
101 shows and presentations that marked the 2007 fashion season in New York, more than one-third used no
black models at all and the rest used just one or two. It
added, "When the fashion caravan moved to London,
Paris, and Milan, the most influential shows . . . made it
appear as if someone had hung out a sign reading: No
Blacks Need Apply."

Some designers and industry observers said the "whiteouts"—a word used by *Washington Post* fashion reporter Robin Givhan, who wrote one of the articles—were merely a matter of "aesthetics," meaning that it's always been the designers' prerogative to choose the kind of models they feel are best suited to embody the message their clothes are meant to convey to the fashion press and the public. Givhan herself noted that the "average person might find it difficult to commiserate with a twenty-one-year-old black girl's complaint that she doesn't get to sashay in expensive clothes before an audience of dilettantes. If modeling is ultimately all about the luck of the gene pool—the right height, the right chin, the right eyes—how does one argue that anyone has a claim on a successful career doing it?"

But there is far more at stake here than just the income and career prospects of a few black models and black-owned modeling agencies. For one thing, the fashion industry is a multibillion-dollar business and, according to *Target Market News*, which tracks the spending patterns of black Americans, black American women annually spend more than $20 billion on apparel. For another, as Givhan pointed out, the fashion industry is based on selling "fantasy, romance, sex appeal and power through their glossy images. They bombard the public with information about what is mainstream and what is subversive, about what is rarefied and what is dross. . . . So what happens if women of color are not included in the conversation about beauty

and femininity. . . . Or when the most influential designers say through their aesthetic choices that dark skin is not
part of their vision?" In other words, there is no difference
between the absence of black models from the runways of
high fashion and the absence of blacks and Hispanics
stalking the gridiron sidelines as head coaches. In all cases,
blacks have been irrationally and prejudicially excluded.

In fact, the striking lack of racial progress, or tokenism,
or even regression so visible in the fashion industry is commonplace in higher education, law, advertising, and other
sectors of society that are gateways to upward mobility and
good salaries. As Calvin Jackson, a sixty-one-year-old sheet
metal worker in Kansas City, Kansas, told a reporter for the
Washington Post, "Things are better, but you still have to
fight for everything you get. You still have to be better at
your job than anyone else. . . . We had trouble here with our
local union. We found out we had the same number of
black journeymen now as we had in 1969. How does that
happen? Nobody knows, but you have your suspicions."

Calvin Jackson's words describe the fundamental characteristic of today's black experience: the complexity of black
progress. Of course, it is a truism that the victories of great
social movements like the twentieth-century civil rights
movement usually produce unforeseen consequences that
undermine the force of some of the gains won. That tension has been especially evident in Black America's efforts
to capitalize on the expanded opportunities of the civil
rights laws and policies. Until the mid-1960s, blacks were

profoundly excluded from even token participation in virtually all sectors of the larger society. For example, in 1965, when the Voting Rights Act was passed, there were just four black members of Congress—one each from Detroit, New York City, Philadelphia, and Chicago. The character of that past exclusion—its having been grounded in law and entrenched social custom—is one reason the progress blacks have made since then has been far from complete: a substantial segment of blacks remain mired in poverty, and even the blacks who have ascended to middle-class status have far fewer assets than their white counterparts. That is substantially due to the ongoing, insidious presence of discrimination in American society—be it housing discrimination that has left many white neighborhoods in cities and suburbs all but officially off-limits to black renters and homebuyers, or white flight from significantly integrated schools, or exclusionary practices in the job market. Finally, for much of the last quarter century, the dominance of the Republican Party and its political conservatism, in the words of one scholar, "all but obliterated support for government policy that was so critical to stabilizing and ensuring the continuance of black progress."[7]

These forces have kept alive and to some extent compounded the negative impact on Black America of the country's Jim Crow past. The result is that even as Black America rightly celebrates the achievements of individual blacks and the rise of a substantial cohort of blacks to middle-class status, it must wrestle with the realities shadowing that progress: that the numerical facts supporting how much progress has been made don't quite justify the acclaim greeting it; that a significant minority of black Americans remain mired in great difficulty; and that the progress achieved during one period can be sharply pared back or disappear altogether in years to come, either through overt bias or the actions of seemingly impersonal forces—a hurricane, an economic recession, a housing downturn—that nonetheless exact a greater toll on blacks than whites.

The devastation wrought in 2005 by Hurricane Katrina in New Orleans and across the Gulf region underscored that reality in the most tragic way. "The storm didn't discriminate" were the words Columbia University scholar Robert C. Lieberman used as the title of his provocative essay in 2006 on what the disaster illuminated about racial poverty and racial politics. "One might think that hurricanes, like other natural phenomena, are equal-opportunity disasters," he began. "They certainly cannot be said to discriminate intentionally. . . . The weather, in short, is color-blind." But while natural events don't discriminate, Lieberman said, Katrina vividly demonstrated that their "destructive effects . . . may not be neutral with respect to race, class or other categories of inequality."[8] Katrina exposed the shocking depth and breadth of black poverty within New Orleans and across the areas of the Gulf most damaged by the storm. In doing so, it revealed how deeply the structural legacy of the discrimination of the past still affects the lives of many blacks and how vulnerable it made them to an unforeseen, negative turn of events.

Even as Hurricane Katrina swept across the Gulf, evidence was accumulating in other parts of the country that another calamity—this one engineered by humans—would likely and disproportionately harm black Americans as well. That was the rise in foreclosures of homes, particularly single-family homes bought by blacks and Hispanics with expensive subprime mortgages (mortgages issued to buyers who don't meet the standard financial criteria for home loans). In 2006, 1.2 million families lost their homes through foreclosure, a number many housing experts expected to increase markedly the following year.[9] By the fall of 2007, the housing crisis was fully engaged: the housing market, overbuilt and overpriced, had softened drastically while many new homeowners were being squeezed by the gap between rising prices for their home's upkeep (such as the cost of oil for heat) and the stagnant wages most workers had endured since the 2001 recession. What made matters worse was that millions of adjustable rate mortgages on homes bought during the height of the housing bubble were due to be recalibrated to sharply higher monthly payments. In the New York metropolitan area, the number of filings for foreclosure involving homes purchased with subprime mortgages during the first nine months of the year had increased by 55 percent over the comparable period in 2006.[10] In the city of Cleveland and several of its surrounding middle-class communities, entire neighborhoods were on the verge of becoming virtual ghost towns as residents lost their homes with no buyers to replace them.

As increasing numbers of borrowers defaulted on their loans, banks and investment banks were forced to write off billions of suddenly shaky mortgage debt, stunning the credit markets. That, in turn, forced the ouster of the chief executives of two financial giants, Merrill Lynch and Citigroup, and roiled financial markets around the world. Experts warned that the shocks were far from over. It was widely estimated that as many as 2 million American homeowners would lose their homes by the middle of 2008.[11]

But the weakness in the housing market, heavily due to the reckless use by banks and other mortgage lenders of subprime mortgages, had already begun to show itself by early 2006. By then, some housing experts were noting sharp increases in foreclosures in predominantly black and Hispanic neighborhoods in and around Chicago, Philadelphia, Atlanta, New York City, and Cleveland. Many whites also took out subprime loans during the housing market frenzy that began in the late 1990s; such loans now make up one-fourth of the entire multitrillion-dollar market. Subprime mortgages produced higher fees than standard mortgages for lenders, and for the lenders, there was almost no risk. Like most loans today, they were soon packaged or "bundled" and sold to fill the loan portfolios of giant financial institutions like Citigroup. But data submitted by lending institutions to the federal Home Mortgage Disclosure Act showed that blacks were more than twice as likely as whites (Hispanics were exactly twice as likely) to have subprime mortgages.[12] The data also showed that more than half of black Americans (and 40 percent of Hispanics) who bought homes in the last decade did so with subprime mortgages.[13] From 2000 to 2003, the percent of blacks filing loan applications for conventional home mortgages declined by 28 percent.[14]

Blacks and Hispanics were more dependent on subprime mortgages partly due to their relatively inferior credit rating, although studies have shown that even blacks with good credit ratings have a more difficult time securing standard mortgages than similarly situated whites. Housing experts also said that two other factors were at work. One factor was the practice by banks of not establishing branches in poor black and Hispanic neighborhoods. Because banks do not have the means to make loans in communities where they have no branches, residents of those neighborhoods have far less opportunity to apply for standard home mortgages. The second factor, according to a 2007 study by the Federal Reserve Bank, was that the biggest mortgage lenders in black and Hispanic neighborhoods were not full-service banks but companies that offered only subprime loans.[15] These companies often aggressively—and unscrupulously—marketed subprime mortgages, convincing renters they could afford to buy a home they actually couldn't and convincing those who already were homeowners to refinance existing, often fixed-rate mortgages—in effect, trading their future mortgage stability for an immediate infusion of cash.

In the end, the devastation produced by today's housing-market collapse—the likelihood that upwards of 2 million people will lose their homes—will almost certainly parallel the catastrophic effect of Hurricane Katrina. By the fall of 2007, overall foreclosure rates were already approaching heights not seen since the Great Depression, and many experts believed the bottoming out of the crisis was still far ahead. Those predictions suggest that Black America will sustain a severe economic setback. Locked out of the standard home mortgage market for decades by both individual bias and institutionalized discrimination, black Americans joined millions of other Americans in the housing market "gold rush" of the past decade. They showed they were as eager as other Americans to pursue the American Dream by securing the one asset that for most Americans represents the bulk of their wealth: a home. They understood that homeownership not only bolsters the economic foundation of individuals and families; it also produces more stable neighborhoods and better schools.

That's why finding a route to owning a home was particularly important for blacks at the lower rungs of the economic ladder. Blacks with solidly middle-class and upper-middle-class incomes had always had high rates of homeownership: in 2000 blacks with annual incomes of $75,000 and above had homeownership rates ranging from 64 to 80 percent (whites' rates at those income levels ranged from 79 to 91 percent). It was the growing numbers of black homeowners with annual incomes between $25,000 and $75,000 since 2000 that pushed the rate up.[16] Unfortunately, blacks (and Hispanics) were overwhelmingly saddled with the riskiest home-buying instrument of all. Some observers estimate that 10 percent of blacks who took out subprime mortgages (compared to 8 percent of Hispanics and 4 percent of whites who did so) will lose their homes by mid-2008.[17]

The effects on Black America will be severe. One outcome will be a marked decline in black homeownership. That rate, which hit a historic high of 50 percent in 2004, had by the fall of 2007 declined nearly two percentage points—pushing it back to its 2000 level.[18] Many of the blacks who lose their homes will never be able to purchase a home again—or never want to. It's also certain that black homeowners with subprime mortgages who escape foreclosure will do so only by meeting much higher monthly payments, leaving them with less money to devote to savings, paying for their children's education, and other necessary expenses. And even blacks who are not directly hit by the housing collapse will likely find it more difficult to purchase homes due to the tightened credit standards.

The blacks that Black America most needs to become homeowners, those with incomes between $25,000 and $50,000, form the class under the greatest financial stress from the economy's overall wage stagnation that has left

more and more middle-class families living in increasingly tough economic circumstances. A recent study conducted by The Center for American Progress, a liberal
think tank, found that dual-income spouses between the
ages of thirty-five and forty-four who had a combined income between $18,000 and $88,000 a year—the middle
60 percent of income distribution—are now significantly
less prepared for a financial emergency than at the beginning of the decade. Families in this range who had at least
three months' worth of their income parked in liquid financial assets had declined from 29 percent in 2001 to
just 18 percent in 2004.[19] That situation, a product of the
economy's lackluster performance in creating new jobs
since the 2001 recession, has forced an overall decline in
median family income. Blacks have been hurt most of all:
their median income in 2005 in actual dollars fell nearly
three times that of both whites and Hispanics.[20] Black
America as a whole will also suffer a marked shrinking of
its already paltry asset base and, as more homes in more
predominantly black neighborhoods go into foreclosure
but continue to stand vacant because there are no buyers
for them, a marked deterioration in the stability of numerous neighborhoods.

The often tenuous nature of black progress starkly exposed
by the housing crisis was also apparent in the wake of the
2001 recession and the jobless recovery that has followed.

The sizable gains blacks had made in household income and in narrowing some gaps between themselves and whites in income during the uninterrupted period of prosperity from 1992 to 2000 were not matched by comparable gains in accumulating financial assets. In fact, because whites were far more heavily invested in stocks and other financial instruments than blacks, the black-white wealth gap has actually increased in recent years. In 2004 the median black household had a paltry net worth of $11,800, just 10 percent of that of the median white household.[21]

Other measures of how wide the wealth gap between blacks and whites stands are equally arresting. More than 20 percent of black households have zero or negative net worth, twice the percentage of white households. Fewer than 4 percent of black households have a net worth of $250,000 or more, compared to 13 percent of white households. Just 1 percent of 13 million black households in the country—about 333,000 households—have a net worth of $500,000 or more. Less than 1 percent of all black households—about 112,000 households—have a net worth of $1 million or more. The number of black households with a net worth of more than $5 million is so small as to be statistically insignificant. By contrast, 5 percent of the nation's white households have more than $500,000 in assets; 6 percent hold $1 million or more in net worth, and more than 1 percent have greater than $5 million in net worth.[22] In all, there are more than 6 million American households with a net worth of $1 million or more.[23] For blacks to approach parity with whites in terms of net worth, the overall wealth of black households would have to increase by $1 trillion; and the number of black billionaires would grow to almost three dozen, up from two, which is the present number.[24] One of those billionaires, entrepreneur Bob Johnson, has noted that blacks are still not a significant presence at the top of many fields that have generated significant wealth for whites: "[T]here are no blacks who own major banks. There are no blacks who own major mining concerns or oil companies. There are no blacks who own major railroads, airlines. There are no blacks who own major department stores, major lumber stores, hardware stores . . . investment banking firms [and] on and on."[25]

These figures offer a sobering corrective to the misleading references to the supposed wealth of Black America that frequently crops up in public discourse. More often than not, those references are based on a few highly visible extremely wealthy black athletes, entertainers, business-men and women, and Black America's "800-billion economy." The latter reference is based on the exhaustive estimates of total black income and black buying power produced by *Target Market News*, the Chicago-based company that analyzes data on the black consumer market. Most often, the total income figure is used without indicating, as the *Target Market News* report does, that the total includes a significant amount that is in fact already *obligated*—both for various government taxes and fees and for such necessities as food, shelter, clothing, children's education, and health care, the cost of which, as already noted, has risen sharply in recent years.[26]

The downturn of the housing market and the battering that black homeowners have suffered from being so heavily dependent on subprime mortgages underscores, just as the 2001 recession and its aftermath did, that blacks remain "perched precariously" on the rungs of American society.[27] They lack significant wealth to start their own businesses; to invest in other businesses and wealth-growing instruments; to pass on wealth and the opportunities it produces to their children, relatives, and civic institutions; to protect themselves in times of personal financial crises; and to safeguard not only against economic downturns but then to use their capital to go bargain-hunting for the assets—homes and stocks and other financial investments—that become available at cheaper prices. Twice in the last decade, when it appeared that blacks were advancing several steps on the escalator of wealth accumulation, a shock to the U.S. economy stripped them of their gains. Coupled with the dramatic increase over the past quarter century in income inequality generally, these setbacks have seriously undermined the occupational and educational gains blacks have made and left them with relatively fewer resources for the future. The luxury cars, spacious homes in good neighborhoods, and other material trappings of the American Dream some black Americans now possess cannot obscure the worrisome possibility that, in its entirety, Black America is standing on quicksand.

3

BLACK AMERICA'S MODERN MIGRATION

Their stories are among the great American success stories—the kind many cite as proof that the very openness of American society, and its eagerness to absorb new talent and enrich its bloodlines inspire even those born at its far reaches to achieve.

The youngest of twelve children, she was born to a sharecropper and domestic servant. Neither of her parents attended school past the seventh grade, a privation not unusual for black Americans trapped in the rural South in the mid-twentieth century. The first home she remembers is a corrugated tin shack propped up on cinderblocks on a hardscrabble patch of east Texas. Her parents had next to nothing—except the one thing she needed: the ambition to see their children become educated and do well. And she did do well: as a scholarship student at New Orleans's historically black Dillard University, as a Fulbright Fellow and a graduate student at Harvard, and in a slew of college and university administrative posts. In 1995, the nation took notice of Ruth Simmons, when Smith College, the storied Massachusetts women's institution, chose her as its first black president. The hurrahs continued to cascade seven years later when she was chosen as Brown University's first black and first woman president.

He was born on the cusp of the Great Depression in Harlem, when the coming hard times for the country meant very hard times for Harlem and all the other enclaves in the North and the South where black Americans lived. His mother was a factory seamstress; his father was someone he knew little of. Until his twentieth year, he seemed destined for an aimless life, a little hustle here, a little hustle there. But the army made him a soldier, his bravery in the Korean War made him a hero, and when he returned from the war to find himself pushing a clothes cart in Manhattan's garment district, he thought, *I've got to do better than this.* So he propelled himself through college and law school and into the vibrant, wheeler-dealer midcentury life of Harlem's black politics. And since the Democrats recaptured the Congress in the 2006 midterm elections, Charles B. Rangel has been chairman of the House Ways and Means Committee, the first black American to hold one of the most powerful posts in the entire federal government.

One might have expected DeVal Patrick's life was going to be like the narrator's in one of Langston Hughes's most famous poems: it would be *no crystal stair,* born as he was into a poor family living in the projects in the wrong part of Chicago. But in his early adolescence, someone noticed that the tough environment he was in could not tamp down his spark of aspiration. He was soon on his way, enrolling in the prestigious Milton Academy, the more prestigious Harvard College, and the even more prestigious Harvard Law School. After a twenty-year career mixing high-level corporate lawyering and high-level government service, DeVal Patrick announced in 2006 that he was running for governor of Massachusetts, the first elective office he had ever sought. In the beginning, the conventional wisdom said: no chance. But in early January 2007, there he was, taking the oath of office in a festive and history-laden ceremony as the first black governor of the Commonwealth of Massachusetts, and only the second black American to be governor of any state of the United States since Reconstruction.

These are black American migration stories. There are millions of them. Each has, at its center, a person whose life and potential have been transformed. In their example is the idea of the rich potential for opportunity that migration offers in America.

Ruth Simmons, Charlie Rangel, and DeVal Patrick were all born in America, like their parents, and they were all migrants. They represent millions of other striving black Americans who have migrated away from the legal and *de facto* restrictions of the Jim Crow decades before 1965 that sharply limited black Americans' upward mobility. No longer satisfied to cap their aspirations at very low levels, this broad band of black Americans has steadily occupied positions once reserved exclusively for whites. The "racial firsts" some of them have recorded show that blacks, with help from White America, have freed themselves to pursue extraordinary achievements throughout American society. Their stories underscore how vibrant and meaningful the concept and reality of the migration dynamic is to the black American experience. From the early to the mid-20th century, migration was a physical act many blacks chose to escape being hemmed in by Southern racism. But the act of movement also bespoke a psychological act, a rebellion against and casting off of the limitations on thought and ambition that the stultifying conventions of American racism imposed. Simply put, the greater opportunity available in the North meant more freedom to think and dream and act as human beings normally do. Blacks' migration expressed their attempt to pursue the American myth—that individual talent and ambition would bring prosperity and a secure place in American society. Blacks' continuing celebration of "racial firsts" today—be it that of a Tiger Woods, a Colin Powell, or an Oprah Winfrey—underscores how motivated they still are by the psychological meaning of migration.

Black Americans' modern pursuit of the freedom to be ambitious was rooted in the U.S. Supreme Court's shameful 1896 decision affirming segregation in *Plessy v. Ferguson*. Anti-black bigotry was so widespread and accepted by both Northern and Southern whites that the ruling was barely noticed in the newspapers of the day. For example, the *New York Times* reported the decision the next day among the railroad news on page three of its second section.[1] But the Court's validation of segregation left the country's 8 million black Americans profoundly exposed: at the time, at least 90 percent of them lived in the South, and nearly half of Southern blacks resided in the rural South. At first blacks followed the counsel of famed black educator Booker T. Washington, the founder of Alabama's Tuskegee Institute (now Tuskegee University). By the mid-1890s, the shrewd, persuasive Washington, born into slavery in 1856, had built Tuskegee from literally a one-room shack into Black America's most powerful organization. More than an educational institution, it was a political machine through which Washington exerted a wide-ranging influence on black affairs across the country. Washington's sway stemmed from his public support for black accommodation to white supremacy and his agreement that workers should subordinate themselves to the captains of capital—those who owned the means of production. Downplaying Tuskegee's academic curriculum, he repeatedly declared that its mission was to produce men skilled in agriculture and the industrial arts and women devoted to elementary school teaching and the "women's work" of home economics. That message had great appeal to two important audiences. It attracted the support of Northern capitalists and the WASP elite who, worried about the continual agitation for better pay and working conditions from America's heavily immigrant industrial working class, wanted a thoroughly docile labor force. Washington's words brought praise from literary giant William Dean Howells and other arbiters of high culture and a steady stream of sizable donations to Tuskegee from the likes of industrialist Andrew Carnegie. And they satisfied white Southern leaders who wanted a thoroughly submissive black population. Washington's public acceptance of the dominance of whites brought the school a measure of protection from the anti-black violence rising throughout the region. The lynching frenzy that would last into the middle of the twentieth century and by some estimates take the lives of nearly 10,000 blacks through illicit mob violence and sham legal proceedings had by the mid-1890s reached the level of 100 per year. It would remain at that level for the bulk of the next two decades. Washington's accommodationism wasn't just a matter of self-aggrandizement or benefiting Tuskegee. He also was acting to shield blacks from even greater devastation.

The year before the Court handed up the *Plessy* decision, Washington gave a speech at the 1895 Cotton States and International Exposition in Atlanta that fully justified white leaders' confidence in his pragmatism. He signaled that blacks would surrender their efforts for political and civil rights in exchange for racial peace and a secure place at the lower reaches of the nation's economic structure. Much of the speech was actually a plea to whites to hire black working men and women and to give black-owned businesses a fair chance to prosper. But, not surprisingly, it was the words he directed to blacks—and a one-sentence pledge to whites—that led to the speech being called "the Atlanta Compromise." To whites, he assured them, "In all things that are purely social, we can be as separate as the fingers, yet one as the hand in all things essential to mutual progress." To blacks, he recommended, "Cast down your bucket where you are—cast it down in making friends in every manly way of the people of all races by whom we are surrounded. . . . Our greatest danger is that in the great leap from slavery to freedom, we may overlook the fact that the masses of us are to live by the productions of our hands, and fail to keep in mind that we shall prosper in proportion as we learn to dignify and glorify common labor, and put brains and skill into the common occupations of life."

His words evoked opposite responses from whites and blacks in the segregated audience. The whites, who had initially jeered the inclusion of a black on the speaking program, began to applaud; blacks, who had initially cheered Washington's appearance, grew stonily quiet. Washington pressed on: "No race can prosper till it learns that there is as much dignity in tilling a field as in writing a poem. It is at the bottom of life we must begin, and not at the top." He concluded that the "wisest among my race understand that the agitation of questions of social equality is the extremist folly, and that progress in the enjoyment of all the privileges that will come to us must be the result of severe and constant struggle rather than of artificial forcing." Harvard University awarded Washington an honorary master's degree within the year.

For most blacks, however, Washington's advice bore bitter fruit. Blacks cast down their buckets, but the well they were drawing from continued to produce little but economic privation and horrific violence. Marooned in a vast sea of cruelty, black Americans began to escape to the North and West. Soon streams of black migrants, many of them nearly illiterate and with little understanding of the ways of urban living, were flooding into those regions' cities with disorienting results for whites and blacks alike. Many of the 1.5 million blacks who left the South during these early years arrived at their destinations with no money, no place to stay, and no job prospects. (Another 5 million blacks left the South between 1940 and 1970.) They had been pushed out of the South by racist oppression; they had also been pulled out by glowing descriptions of better opportunities that appeared in black Northern newspapers that enjoyed wide circulation in Southern black communities. The floodtide produced two immediate consequences that had a lasting impact on Black America's fortunes. It hardened the intentions of a small band of black and white racial radicals to attack the problem of racial discrimination, ultimately leading to the founding of the National Association for the Advancement of Colored People (NAACP). And it compelled the tiny black middle class and working class of the urban North and their allies among whites to establish a variety of social service organizations in a desperate effort to reduce the social chaos. The National Urban League was formed in 1910 in New York City expressly to school the migrants crowding into that city's black neighborhoods in the requirements of modern life—and to get them jobs.

As the need for cheap labor outside the South intensified during World War I and beyond, the black migrations grew apace. Chicago saw its black population swell from 44,000 in 1910 to 234,000 by 1930. In Detroit, the black population expanded exponentially, too, from a shade above 5,700 in 1910 to more than 120,000 by 1930. Indeed, one way of tracking the many routes of the black migrations during the middle decades of the twentieth century is to map the establishment of National Urban League chapters (called "affiliates"). Until World War I, the league had only one office in New York. In 1916 the Detroit affiliate was opened. By 1922 there were fifteen more Urban League affiliates in such cities as Chicago, Pittsburgh, St. Louis, and Los Angeles.

The black migrations were the making of twentieth-century Black America. As author Nicholas Lemann notes, they constituted "one of the largest and most rapid mass internal movements of people in history—perhaps *the* [his emphasis] greatest not caused by the immediate threat of execution or starvation. In sheer numbers it outranks the migration of any other ethnic group ... to this country."[2] They brought a critical mass—ultimately, close to half of the country's total black population—out of the feudal environment of the rural South, a region where they had been allowed almost no acquaintance with the attitudes and implements of modern life. Despite the presence of nearly a hundred black colleges spread throughout the South (their enrollments were always relatively small), most Southern blacks could gain little formal schooling beyond the sixth grade. The suffocating grip of the sharecropping system, which effectively re-created the antebellum plantation system, saw to it that black boys and girls were put to work in the fields years before the onset of adolescence. Before migrating to the North, many black Southerners had little experience with money, indoor plumbing, or the rudiments of personal hygiene. And they had scant experience with any kind of collective political action. The migration experience changed that. It exposed millions of blacks to a mass society: to a world of education through the North's public school systems and its museums and libraries; to a world of information through the news media and movies and radio; to rubbing shoulders, sometimes bruisingly, with the wildly diverse throng crowding urban America; to the cities' subways, streetcars, buses, and cars that constituted the modern means of transportation; to the specialized industrial machinery of the modern era; to relatively decent medical care available in the large urban public hospitals; and to relatively decent housing.

For many new arrivals, the exposure was often filled with considerable discrimination, poverty, and bitterness: the nation's urban black ghettos were created, after all, in the North, not in the South. Nor were black Southern migrants mere empty vessels who willingly or unthinkingly accepted the efforts of the dominant white society or the black church and black social service organizations to impose conventional middle-class norms on them.[3] But for the first time in American history, the migration experience enabled millions of black Americans to freely congregate with a mass of fellow black Americans and to publicly act and speak their minds on racial issues without fear of violent retaliation from whites.

Moreover, blacks in the North had what blacks in the South did not: the right to vote. As more and more blacks left the South, they used that fundamental marker and tool of citizenship to force the white-controlled urban political machines of the North to share more resources with them. And, beginning with Franklin Roosevelt's administration, Northern blacks used their growing voting power to press the national political structure of both Democratic and Republican parties to repudiate legalized racism and ensure that their brethren in the South could exercise their civil rights, too.

In other words, blacks used the greater freedom they found in the North to funnel more resources into the fight against anti-black bigotry in the South, too. That is one way the migration dynamic of black Americans differed from that of white ethnic Americans—those of Italian,

Jewish, Irish, Slavic, and Eastern-European descent. For all the bigotry white ethnic immigrants and their descendants encountered in the United States, the millions of Europeans who came to America in great waves from the 1880s to the 1920s left behind the suffocating oppression that had driven them to migrate. In America, their labor was needed to fuel the nation's expanding economic might. The trade unions they formed would over time win them decent working conditions and better wages. And the disciplined political machines of the urban North they supported provided an easily understood *quid pro* quo— votes in exchange for civil service jobs, civil service contracts, and other forms of patronage, including outright graft—that created a kind of safety net ensuring that most of them would not endure extreme poverty. So, too, did the Northern variant of Jim Crow that for decades barred blacks from the unions and most municipal jobs.

At first, America's black Southern migrants had no such help; and they had not migrated to a new country but to a different part of the same country. Through family members and friends who remained in the South, and news coverage of black life in the South in dozens of widely read black newspapers, black Northerners were fully aware of how little conditions in the South were changing. Finally, while the migrants' new home offered a measure of opportunity significantly greater than could be found in the South, Northern-style discrimination was always close at hand—some of it dealt by white ethnic immigrants whose

American roots were far shallower than blacks. Everywhere, white racism, whether by law or custom, assigned black Americans to the lowest rungs—or no rungs at all—of the social-economic ladder. In the South, it was a matter of law, backed by extralegal violence. In the North, the private sector—with banks, businesses, and real estate in the lead—was racial discrimination's primary enforcer.[4] Black Southern migrants had crossed a boundary, the Mason-Dixon Line, but black Americans' physical and legal migration away from discrimination and toward freedom was far from complete. That reality became especially vivid during the two world wars the United States fought—"to make the world safe for democracy." On the one hand, the country's need for labor to staff defense industry plants, and for men to staff the military dramatized how much a part of America black Americans were. On the other, blacks endured ceaseless bigotry even during wartime. The vivid contrasts during these national emergencies between white Americans' rhetorical boasts about liberty and the reality that blacks faced every day stoked their determination to move ahead to find their own freedom and opportunity. They understood they could only do so by moving white Americans away from their commitment to legalized racism and toward an acceptance of racial equality.

The gathering of a critical mass of blacks outside the South by the 1930s is what made that objective possible.

The collective energy and self-confidence that blacks derived from grappling with the urban experience, expressed so dramatically in the 1920s in both the flowering of black culture known as Negro Renaissance and the flamboyant black nationalist movement of Marcus Garvey, was channeled in the 1930s into supporting a patient but unrelenting legal attack on segregation. Historically speaking, it was no accident that, during that decade, Charles Hamilton Houston, dean of the Howard University Law School, formed what became known as the Brain Trust, a group of veteran lawyers and law school students (including one of Houston's best students, Thurgood Marshall) who would plot the legal strategy that ultimately led to the 1954 Supreme Court decision in *Brown v. Board of Education of Topeka*.

There was much to overcome, and, contrary to the conventional wisdom, the impact of racism on the legislation of the New Deal would be part of the problem down to the present day. That legislation could not have passed without the approval of Southern legislators who, because of their seniority, controlled the key congressional committees. The price they demanded was the policies' total obeisance to Jim Crow. "As a result, *every* [emphasis in the original] piece of New Deal legislation was carefully crafted to exclude blacks from coverage, or failing that, to delegate to the states [that] authority. . . . [T]hroughout the postwar era, millions of African Americans fell through the holes in the American social safety net that were deliberately put there to allow them to pass through."[5] This institutional-

ization of racism in federal policies continued after World
War II with such acts as the GI Bill and the Federal Housing Administration mortgage lending program, which
established an entrenched structural inequality that still
operates today: the homeownership gap between blacks
and whites and the concentration of black homeowners in
the subprime mortgage market are just two if its legacies.[6]

Nonetheless, from that point on, Black America would
have legalized segregation on the run because their presence was highly visible—and contentious—in the North's
most populous cities and industrial centers. Their efforts
forced a crucial segment of America's national white leadership in the courts, politics, labor unions, higher education, business, religion, and philanthropy to work to
modernize America's racial posture. Some did it willingly,
some grudgingly. All were responding to the imperative
of powerful national and global developments. The emergencies of the Great Depression and the fight against the
brutal doctrines of Japan, Germany, and later, the Soviet
Union demanded that the United States ultimately shed
not only its *de jure* apartheid but also its more overt *de
facto* racism. Equality of opportunity had to be extended
across the color line. As the twentieth century proceeded,
it would be White America that accommodated itself to
the black freedom struggle.

That accommodation began to speed up right after
World War II, as blacks fought on the labor front to keep
the job gains in industry they had made during the war
years. Slowly through the late 1940s and 1950s, American

industries responded, and black white-collar workers began appearing in the middle ranks of American corporations. However, the progress was best dramatized when officially sanctioned racism was eliminated in two sectors of society that were central to America's sense of self. Jackie Robinson's breaking the color barrier in Major League Baseball in 1947 put black Americans back on the field to play a sport* that writers and average Americans agreed displayed quintessential elements of the American character. A year later, President Truman's executive order desegregating the military acknowledged what had always been true—that black Americans were critical to the defense of the country. If America was prepared to ask black Americans to die for their country, the moral obligation to let them live freely in that same country became unavoidable. More practically, the opening of the peacetime military, enabling millions of black men and women over the next several decades to gain practical skills, steady employment, and an income on a short- or long-term basis, was an invaluable boon to Black America.

The victory of the civil rights movement in the 1960s completed the first stage of Black America's recovery from the devastating consequences of the *Plessy* decision: it enabled a substantial number of blacks to expand their

---

*Blacks had played baseball throughout the late nineteenth century but were officially banned from the sport in 1897.

horizons and pursue their ambitions across American society. In turn, that produced a different kind of black migration populated by a different kind of migrant. These black migrants had formal educational credentials and job skills, and they had a confidence gained from a movement that had changed the nation.

This was the black opportunity class. Overwhelmingly, most were from working-class, not middle-class, families. But the civil rights movement's opening of American society and their own individual ambitions had put them in position to show that the Horatio Alger myth could apply to those on the other side of the color line, too. Blacks could aspire to high achievement and extraordinary status. Equally important, they could also expand the ranks of the middle class. More than 25 percent of the nearly 15 million blacks in today's labor force are professionals or hold mid- or senior-level managerial positions, and another 25 percent occupy lower-level white-collar jobs, the same percentage as whites.[7]

One other factor was critical to their success, to their migration from the fringes to the center of the American mainstream: affirmative action. This was the policy developed during the administrations of Lyndon Johnson and Richard Nixon to give special consideration to blacks to correct for both past discrimination and contemporary bias. Those deliberate, color-conscious steps taken from the mid-1960s onward by local, state, and federal government agencies, private companies, and, most of all, top-ranked colleges and universities are responsible for the demographic reality the census data now shows: the peopling of more and more sectors of American society with growing numbers of blacks, white women, and other people of color. Affirmative action, after the civil rights victories, propelled this next stage of black migration, enabling significant numbers of blacks to move up the rungs of the nation's occupational and income ladder.

But the extension of opportunity past the old boundaries of tokenism—in which the presence of just one or two blacks amid an enrollment of thousands was deemed sufficient to declare a white institution "integrated"—provoked a virulent reaction against affirmative action.

Conservatives, some centrists, and even some progressives have declared that affirmative action is unfair, that it violates the sacrosanct principle of scrupulously fair competition and selection based purely on merit. Such a charge is disingenuous at best. It ignores the fact that there are two kinds of affirmative action. One is affirmative action for blacks and other people of color and white women. In much of the public discourse, this kind of affirmative action is largely deemed unfair, or at best, problematic. The other kind of affirmative action is the preferential treatment reserved for whites. This kind of affirmative action, embedded in the very structure of American society by the long, pervasive denial of opportunity to others, is rarely described in those terms—even when the educational record of one president of the United States, George W. Bush, offers unmistakable proof of how it operates.

During the 2000 presidential campaign, the *New York Times* published several lengthy profiles of George W. Bush and Al Gore. In writing about the former, the paper noted that during prep school at Phillips Andover Academy, the alma mater of his father and grandfather, the future president was "a mediocre student" whose grades and college entrance examination scores ranked him far below most of his classmates.[8] Nonetheless, he was admitted to Yale, which was the alma mater of his father and grandfather as well. The *Times* described Bush's good fortune as an example of the "helping hand" that benefits alumni children of prominent parents at Yale and other highly sought-after colleges and universities. As an undergraduate, George W. continued the pattern he had shown in secondary school: he earned mediocre grades and showed little, if any, interest in the major events of the day on campus or off. Yet a few years after graduation from Yale, he was admitted to Harvard Business School.[9] The *Times* also reported that at Phillips Andover and Yale, George W. showed a trait that would be much remarked upon throughout his political career—the ability to cultivate a large group of loyal friends, to make people like him and trust him.

One reader, noting that Bush, as governor of Texas, enthusiastically supported the successful challenge that eliminated affirmative action for Texas's state university system, wrote that she found it "paradoxical that [Bush] is himself the beneficiary of one of the most insidious forms of the practice of the 'legacy' system through which the children of the elite are admitted into competitive schools and colleges, fraternities and private clubs. . . . For the white and the rich, it was called a 'helping hand'; for minorities, it is called affirmative action and is in danger."[10]

In fact, preferential treatment is a well-established principle of American society, in both its good and bad forms. The Jim Crow laws and customs that ruled much of American society until the mid-1960s were an obvious and invidious form. The constellation of federal programs that began with Franklin Roosevelt's New Deal raised millions of poor and working-class whites to middle-class status—laced as they were with anti-black bigotry—and exemplified the good that government could achieve in directing benefits to particular classes of citizens.

Today, the controversy over affirmative action has focused almost exclusively on admissions policies at the most prestigious public universities. As the case involving affirmative action at the University of Michigan illustrated, these highly selective and highly sought-after institutions offer easy targets for its opponents to exert pressure through lawsuits or voter referenda to eliminate such programs. The University of Michigan was a particularly important target for the antiaffirmative-action forces because among the nation's thirty highest-ranked universities, Michigan enrolled the largest number of black students—1,887 out of a total of more than 45,000 students—in the fall of 2006. Only 3 other highly ranked universities enroll more than 1,000 students.

Daniel Golden explored the hypocrisy of many antiaffirmative-action arguments in his 2006 book, *The Price of Admission: How America's Ruling Class Buys Its Way into Elite Colleges—and Who Gets Left Outside the Gates.* He specified the multiple "preferences of privilege" that "ensure each fresh generation of upper-class families—regardless of intelligence or academic qualifications—access to premier colleges whose alumni hold disproportionate sway on Wall Street and in Fortune 500 companies, the media, Congress, and the judiciary." Golden said this context, largely missing from the public discussion about affirmative action, enables critics of affirmative action in higher education admissions to depict it as unfair to whites, when "the truth is the reverse. The number of whites enjoying preference far outweighs the number of minorities aided by affirmative action."[11]

In other words, affirmative action, informally and indeed murkily characterized by such monikers as "the old boys' network" and "the helping hand," has long been a traditional mechanism of advancement among whites, wealthy and poor. When it comes to college admissions practices, critics of affirmative action for people of color have long accepted the principle that led to George W. Bush's admission to Yale and Harvard Business School: for white applicants, a host of reasons, including family pedigree or wealth, can trump a strict adherence to test scores, grade point averages, and other supposedly objective standards of merit. These critics seek to remove "the helping hand" for people of color in order to limit the field of competitors for positions of affluence and status in the society.

Black Americans have no doubt of the validity of affirmative action, or their need for it. Since its implementation in the 1960s, surveys have consistently shown that large numbers of blacks continue to believe that discrimination in higher education and in the workplace remains at high levels. In sharp contrast, whites by and large do not. For example, in the November 2006 midterm elections, two-thirds of Michigan's white electorate voted to eliminate the state's affirmative action policy. But 87 percent of the state's black voters (who comprise less than 15 percent of the electorate) supported its continuation. A 2007 Gallup Poll asked respondents: If two equally qualified students—one white, one black—applied for admission to a major university, would both have an equal chance of admission or would one have an advantage? Forty-eight percent of whites said both students would have an equal chance and another 26 percent said the black student would be favored. By contrast, 61 percent of blacks polled said the white student would be favored and just 5 percent of blacks said the black student would be favored. When Gallup put the same question to only those blacks and whites who themselves had graduated from college, 41 percent of whites said both students would have an equal chance of admission and another 31 percent said the black student would be favored, but only 25 percent of black college alumni said both students would have an equal chance. Exactly two-thirds of blacks, 67 percent, said the white student would be favored, while only 3 percent said the black student would have the advantage.[12]

These recent polls reinforce earlier findings of high levels of black support for affirmative action, such as one conducted in 2001 by the National Urban League. It found that blacks at all ages and income levels—by percentages that ranged from 81 to 92 percent—said affirmative action was still necessary in higher education and in the workplace.[13] Those majorities even included blacks at very high levels on the occupational ladder, as scholar Susan D. Toliver found in her examination of a particular group of high-achieving blacks. Toliver conducted one of the few book-length studies of the attitudes about work, family, and the status of blacks in America that drew from a large group of black mid- and senior-level corporate managers working for Fortune 100 companies. Her subjects, numbering nearly 200, were a very select group: three-quarters were college graduates and nearly all had attended college for some period of time. More than half had gone on to graduate school; just under half held graduate degrees. More than 70 percent of their spouses were college graduates, and nearly half of the spouses had also attended graduate school for some time. Most of the subjects lived in the suburbs, placed their children in private schools, and vacationed generally two to four times a year. More than 70 percent of the managers had grown up in blue-collar families; the rest were from middle-class backgrounds.[14] Their support of affirmative action was unwavering. One responded, "Affirmative action is good and necessary. Without it, we wouldn't have gotten this far." Another manager said affirmative action was still needed "to keep people honest." Still a third added, "I'm very strongly in favor of affirmative action. I feel it's essential and I feel it's a real setback that these programs have been cut."[15]

Those sentiments were echoed more recently by Bob Johnson, entrepreneur, founder of Black Entertainment Television (BET), and America's first black billionaire. "I definitely favor affirmative action," he told the *Washington Post*. "I favor affirmative action to the point that I think there should be some way of measuring affirmative action with quotas and other forms of accountability, that says if you benefit from the government, you have an affirmative obligation to meet certain goals in the way this money is being allocated or being spent or the way you're providing job opportunities. I'm saying you have an obligation to go out and find people, and they're out there. I know because I go out and I find them. So you can't say you can't find them."[16]

By huge majorities, black Americans understand that affirmative action is an instrument of opportunity and mobility, a means of engaging in a different kind of migration experience. Their support for it was partly driven by the desire to climb higher up the economic ladder. But it involved something more intangible—a desire by blacks to move deeper into the American mainstream and to take hold of the full measure of their American heritage.

The signs of that pursuit were apparent by 1980, as the first wave of black baby boomers, men and women who had graduated from college in the late 1960s and early 1970s, reached their full maturity and were making their presence felt in their careers. By then, some 40 percent of blacks in the workforce held white-collar jobs, compared to 52 percent of whites and 32 percent of Hispanics. As blacks moved into the middle and upper reaches of the country's workforce, they began to form a large constellation of their own professional associations on the outside and inside of the white institutions they were working for. These included the National Association of Black Manufacturers, the National Association of Black Accountants, the Organization of Black Airline Pilots, and others.[17] Although much more sober in their dress and rhetoric than the black student organizations on white college campuses of the time, it's clear in hindsight that they had the same purpose regarding blacks' interaction with the American system: to aid the movement of the black opportunity class into the American mainstream. Black student organizations and black studies departments did not become, as some predicted in the turbulent years of the late 1960s, enclaves of "separatism," producing black graduates who would contribute only turmoil to the larger society, and

"black caucuses" inside corporations proved far from intent on wrecking the companies.

The most dramatic example of the post-civil-rights-
movement black migration experience occurred in the
political arena. There, black Americans quickly showed
they fully understood the importance of mixing in with
the political mainstream. President Kennedy once said, "I
like politics. It's how things get done." Once the Voting
Rights Act was passed in 1965, blacks set about using the
political system to get things done. In 1964, there were
only 350 black elected officials in the United States, including just 4 blacks in the House of Representatives. By
1970, with blacks in the South in secure possession of the
vote, that national total had increased to 1,469; by 1980,
the number jumped to more than 4,900; and by 2000,
it exceeded 9,040. Currently, there are a total of 43 members of the Congressional Black Caucus (there are 20
members of the Congressional Hispanic Caucus).[18] Black
Americans are now almost completely spread across the
full range of elected and appointed political offices in
America. Symbolically speaking, one example above all
others demonstrates the vigor with which blacks pursued
politics as soon as the Voting Rights Act destroyed the
barriers to their voting in the South. That was the skillful
campaign for the Democratic presidential nomination
mounted in 1972 by Representative Shirley Chisholm,
then a little-known congresswoman from Brooklyn's pre-

dominantly black Bedford-Stuyvesant district and an
outsider even among the predominantly male black political establishment. Despite not being taken seriously
by most of the political establishment and the media,
Chisholm campaigned across the country, won delegates,
and pursued the nomination at the Democratic National
Convention until she conceded to the superior delegate
strength of the eventual nominee, South Dakota senator
George McGovern.

Not until the presidency of Bill Clinton did these
developments—the maturing of black political activity and
of the black opportunity class—begin to be appreciated.
During the presidencies of Ronald Reagan and George
H. W. Bush, Black America's established political and civil
rights leadership often seemed uncertain about how to
combat the dominant political conservatism of the time,
which, at least rhetorically, was fortified by GOP leaders'
claims that a "new" black conservative phalanx of intellectuals and political operatives would soon sweep the main-
line civil rights forces into the dustbin of history. Their
racial hostility was clear. Ronald Reagan opened his 1980
campaign for the White House with a speech extolling
states' rights in Philadelphia, Mississippi, site of the infamous, and then still unsolved, 1964 murder of the three
civil rights workers. Eight years later, Bush, running for
president and badly trailing Massachusetts governor
Michael Dukakis in the polls, latched on to William Horton, a black convict who had raped and murdered a white
woman while on furlough from a Massachusetts state

prison during Dukakis's tenure. The Bush camp renamed Horton "Willie," which no one had ever called him, said he represented Dukakis's misguided crime policies, and rode the ensuing racially driven controversy to electoral victory.

In the 1980s, black and white progressive forces seemed in disarray, incapacitated by the political flexibility and ruthlessness of the Republicans. But in hindsight, it's apparent that blacks were gaining important experience in the mechanics of high-level political action. In 1984 and 1988, the Reverend Jesse Jackson, whose black leftist activism sprang from the 1960s civil rights campaigns, mounted—with a scant organizational structure in traditional terms—presidential campaigns that forced both parties to pay attention. In 1984 in Chicago, Harold Washington, a veteran black politician, tamed the combat-zone politics that had always been the local style to become that city's first black mayor. In New York City in 1989, David Dinkins, another black old-school politician, wrestled the Democratic nomination for mayor from incumbent Ed Koch, further proving that black politicians could craft multiracial coalitions even under the difficult task of battling a popular and powerful white officeholder. That same year, Doug Wilder, a courtly and savvy black Virginia Democrat, was elected governor of his state, prompting a slew of articles in the mainstream media layered with reconciliation-of-the-races sentimentality.

Ronald H. Brown, however, wasn't playing politics for the sentimental value. He was the man who played a crucial role in crafting the strategy for the victory of Bill Clinton in 1992, and he, too, was a classic figure of Black America's modern black migration.

Born in Harlem to middle-class parents—his father was manager of the community's famed Hotel Theresa—Brown grew up in material circumstances unusual for blacks at the time. He enrolled at Middlebury College in the late 1950s, returned to New York to attend law school, and, after a stint as a social worker in an impoverished Lower East Side neighborhood, joined the National Urban League. His talent shone brightly and he was soon sent to head the league's Washington governmental office. In the early 1980s, Brown made the kind of career move that had been a staple of white upper-middle-class life for decades but had only just become available to blacks. He went into the private sector as a rainmaker at a powerful Washington law firm. By the time he won election as the first black chairman of the Democratic National Committee in early 1989, he was regularly being described in the media as "an influential Washington lawyer." His campaign against four competitors was so deft that when the time came to cast their ballots, the committee's 403 members dispensed with voting and elected him by acclamation. "We all wish we were skilled enough to run a campaign like that," said one committee member from the South. What made Brown's smooth election doubly striking—and significant—was that the year before, he had been Jesse Jackson's convention manager at the Democratic National Convention. He was one of several black political operatives who gained crucial experience working in the Jackson camp before moving deeper into mainstream political work.

Brown's election as DNC chairman further confirmed the power of the migration that had been occurring throughout Black America and showed how that migration was playing out on the broader stage of American society. Three years later, the party that had been battered by losing three consecutive presidential contests would be toasting its new occupant of the White House; and Ron Brown, having been offered his choice of cabinet posts by President Clinton, chose to be secretary of commerce because he understood that the new global economy had transformed the post into one of enormous potential political and economic power.

Bill Clinton's presidency, encompassing the longest sustained period of economic growth the nation had enjoyed since World War II, solidified Black America's modern migration. For the first time in twelve years, a sympathetic administration was in office, and its symbolic openness was matched by a record number of black appointments to cabinet, subcabinet, and other high-level bureaucratic posts as well as support for private-sector ventures of black entrepreneurs. Simultaneously, the booming economy was filling the wallets of the new black middle class and stable working class. It was a reign of good fortune that would, just before the so-called long boom came to an end, even open the low-wage job market at the very bottom of the job ladder to poor young black males. In 1999, just as the federal Department of Labor was reporting that the black unemployment rate had fallen to a post–World War II low of 7 percent, the National Bureau of Economic Research, the Cambridge, Massachusetts-based think tank that serves as the official arbiter of whether the economy is in a recession or not, published a study that showed the reason for the decline.

The national study of more than 300 metropolitan areas found that black males, ages 16 to 24, with a high school education or less, were working in greater numbers and earning bigger paychecks than ever before. This meant that the long period of prosperity was bestowing its benefits in significant fashion to those at the bottom of the economic and occupational ladder. The other point to be made was that these young, poorly educated males, a group that had endured double-digit unemployment since the 1960s—were taking those jobs. The study noted an ancillary effect of the greater employment among poor blacks: levels of reported crime had fallen most sharply in those metropolitan areas where declines in joblessness had been greatest.[19]

For a brief moment, the decrease in the black unemployment rate (the white unemployment rate declined to 4.2 percent) made it seem as if Black America were on the verge of a new period of upward mobility, one that would give bootstraps to more of its poor so they could use them to pull themselves out of poverty. Yet it was striking that the news drew relatively little notice. After all, for years conservatives, centrists, and even some progressives had been declaring that the black poor were trapped in a "culture of poverty," driven by their poor education and social habits to denigrate the intrinsic value of work and the importance of, if necessary, starting at the bottom of the occupational ladder. Now they had shown that they well understood the value of work and were eager for the chance, even if it meant starting at the very bottom. E. J. Dionne, a *Washington Post* columnist, did note the development. He wrote that it indicated that "those who argued for years that the plight of the poor owed more to what was wrong with the economy than to what was wrong with the poor have been proved right." Political science scholar Jennifer L. Hochschild told the *New York Times:* "Poor blacks never lost faith in work, education and individual effort. What's different now is that they can do something about it."

These comments recall a story that appeared in the *New York Times* in June 1992, when the economic boom of the decade was just beginning. It told the story of the Disney Company holding interviews that month in the predominantly black Los Angeles neighborhood of South-Central for 200 summer jobs at Disneyland for young people ages 17 to 22. According to the article, it was a goodwill gesture born of the riots the previous summer that had made the neighborhood's name synonymous with urban despair. Disneyland is 30 miles from South-Central, so perhaps the company wasn't expecting much of a turnout. But when company officials arrived at the First A.M.E. Church there, they found "more than 600 young men and women, many in coats and ties or dresses" waiting for them. The officials "were taken aback. America has been bombarded with television images of the youth of South-Central Los Angeles throwing bricks, looting stores, beating up innocent motorists. The Disneyland staff who interviewed the job applicants . . . found a different neighborhood. 'They were wonderful kids, outstanding kids,' said . . . a spokesman for Disneyland. 'We didn't know they were there.'"[20]

Among the black poor, which much of the rest of America doesn't know is "there," is a group of black Americans still waiting for the chance to make their migration to opportunity. The black poor, as a group, lost the wherewithal to do something about their joblessness as the economic recession hit and was followed by a long jobless recovery in the first years of this decade. Those developments, along with the current housing crisis, have placed a high and wide barrier in the path of Black America's unfinished journey.

4

NO CHOICE
Blacks and the GOP

THINGS WERE GOING TO BE DIFFERENT NOW, KEN
Mehlman, chairman of the Republican National Committee, told the national convention of the NAACP in
July 2005. The Republican Party was going to be different when it came to pursuing black voters. It was going to
go after them with black and white candidates and policies that Black America would find appealing.

This was the message that Mehlman, a Washington
lawyer who had managed President Bush's 2004 re-
election campaign, had been assiduously pushing before
numerous black groups since taking the RNC post at the
start of 2005. He was a man on a mission. He knew that
if the GOP was going to build up its tiny bloc of black

support, he had to overcome a decades-long record of policy proposals, congressional and presidential actions, and public pronouncements most blacks considered evidence of Republican indifference, if not outright racism. That sentiment was particularly widespread within the NAACP, whose relationship with President Bush was one of mutual hostility. In the 2000 election, the NAACP's nonprofit—and thus officially nonpartisan—status did not prevent its political arm from running two related "issues" ads that were clearly anti-Bush just before the November election. One ad urged viewers to demand that Bush, still governor of Texas, reverse his opposition to hate-crimes laws being considered by the state legislature. The second recalled the notorious 1998 murder in Texas of James Byrd Jr., a black man who was beaten by several white men, chained to the back of their pickup truck, and dragged for three miles to his death. The ads were shown in ten states containing the country's largest numbers of black voters.[1] Amid the bitter controversies that erupted over the election's voting irregularities, top NAACP officials were among those pressing hardest to dispute its results, and they continued to criticize the administration sharply throughout its first term.

For his part, President Bush repeatedly declined the organization's invitation to address its annual convention, and many felt he would become the first post-World-War-II president never to speak before the NAACP. (In 2006 he accepted an invitation to speak before the organization.) The bitterness culminated in a scathing attack on the president's policies by NAACP chairman Julian

Bond during the organization's 2004 convention. Within weeks, the Internal Revenue Service announced that it was investigating whether the group had violated federal rules barring tax-exempt organizations from political advocacy. The investigation came to nothing, except to remind many blacks of the bare-knuckled tactics the GOP had been using against Black America since the 1960s.

In July 2005, therefore, Ken Mehlman, who had already gained high marks for his sincerity from even those skeptical of the GOP, was candid. He apologized for the party's long use of the "Southern strategy"—successfully employing coded racist appeals in order to wean white voters who had traditionally voted Democratic to the Republican ballot. Invoking the GOP's nineteenth-century past as the party of Lincoln, Mehlman told the convention delegates, "No matter how many elections Republicans win, the Republican Party will not be whole again until more African Americans come back home."[2]

If the GOP's intent was sincere, as Mehlman claimed, it had a lot to atone for. For the GOP's deliberate turning away from Black America did not start with President George W. Bush or even with President Reagan. It was rooted in the 1960 presidential contest between Republican Richard M. Nixon and Democrat John F. Kennedy.

In defeat, Nixon had secured 32 percent of the black vote against John F. Kennedy's 68 percent. That continued the pattern of Republican presidential candidates garnering respectable support from blacks even after Roosevelt's New Deal programs shielding the poor from the worst effects of the Great Depression had brought about a massive shift in black presidential voting patterns. Before the 1930s, blacks had been heavily committed to the Republican Party, both in remembrance of Lincoln and Theodore Roosevelt, and because the rise of white supremacy in the South was fostered and maintained by the Democratic Party's southern faction of representatives and senators and state and local officeholders. But blacks' political allegiance began to shift during the Great Depression, a result of Franklin Roosevelt's personal magnetism and New Deal policies, and, perhaps equally so, Eleanor Roosevelt's advocacy of greater government aid to the poor and her obvious commitment to the cause of racial equality. As a result, from 1936 to 1956, the black vote for the Democratic presidential candidate ranged from 61 to 77 percent. The comparable Republican figures were from 24 to 40 percent.[3]

Some analysts, arguing that the Republicans' 1960 civil rights plank was actually better than the Democrats', believed Nixon would have done much better that November but for the famous phone call that swung the black vote decisively to JFK. In October, less than three weeks before the election, Martin Luther King Jr., already recognized as Black America's most prominent civil rights leader, had been arrested in Georgia on a traffic technicality: he was still using his Alabama license, although by then he had lived in Georgia for three months. A swift series of moves by the state's segregationist power structure resulted in King being sentenced to four months of hard labor on a Georgia chain gang. He was quickly spirited away to the state's maximum security prison, and many of his supporters, fearing for his life, urgently called both the Nixon and Kennedy camps for help. Nixon, about to campaign in South Carolina in the hopes of capturing that state's normally solid Democratic vote, took no action. Kennedy took swift action. He made a brief telephone call to a frantic Coretta Scott King, speaking in soothing generalities and telling her, "If there is anything I can do to help, please feel free to call on me."

It's likely that Kennedy did not at that moment realize the political implications of the call. Ever the pragmatist, he had resisted the pleas of several aides throughout the campaign that he take bolder public stands on civil rights issues. The telephone call came because one aide caught him late at night after a hard day of campaigning and staff meetings as he was about to turn in. The aide, Harris Wofford, pitched it as just a call to calm King's fearful spouse. Kennedy replied, "What the hell. That's a decent thing to do. Why not? Get her on the phone."

King was soon released, unharmed, due to a groundswell of pressure directed by blacks and whites in numerous quarters toward Georgia officials (Robert F. Kennedy himself, who was managing his brother's campaign, called the judge who sentenced King to prison). At the time, the white media paid little attention to the call, which suited the Kennedys fine. But it likely transformed the black vote. King's father, Martin Luther King Sr., a dominating,

fire-and-brimstone preacher with wide influence throughout Black America, had, like many black Southerners, always been a Republican and until that moment had said
he couldn't vote for Kennedy because he was a Catholic.
The day his son was released from prison, the elder King
thundered from the pulpit of his famed Ebenezer Baptist
Church in Atlanta: "I had expected to vote against Senator
Kennedy because of his religion. But now he can be my
president, Catholic or whatever he is. . . . He has the
moral courage to stand up for what he knows is right. I've
got all my votes and I've got a suitcase, and I'm going to
take them up there and dump them in his lap."[4] From that
moment, JFK's bond with blacks, despite his initial tepid
support for the movement, was sealed. His assassination,
less than six months after proposing what became the
Civil Rights Act of 1964, cemented his place of honor
among blacks: for years afterward, inexpensive commemo-
rative plates imprinted with his likeness were ubiquitous
in the homes of blacks across the country. And when his
successor, Lyndon Baines Johnson, took up the civil rights
cause and pushed both the Civil Rights Act and the Voting Rights Act through Congress, black voters moved in
massive numbers to the Democratic Party.

The GOP helped with the move. In the wake of
Nixon's defeat, it ran off its numerically respectable
core of black voters as power within its ranks shifted
from the once-dominant bloc of eastern and midwest-
ern moderate-conservatives, which had always taken a

moderate-progressive stance on civil rights issues. The new power bloc came from states in the far West and on the southern rim. Led by Arizona senator Barry Goldwater, they were hostile to the eastern establishment and to the civil rights movement. The potential for the Republican Party to make significant inroads in the South by appealing to segregationist sentiment had been apparent even before the Kennedy-Nixon contest, as *Time* magazine's famed correspondent Theodore H. White noted in his pathbreaking book on the election, *The Making of the President 1960*. The Southern white, he wrote, "knows himself bound to a Democratic Party that, in the North, is increasingly responsive to Negro pressure for intervention in domestic Southern affairs." That meant, White went on to say, that the Republicans could seek political gain in the region "by a forthright Republican abandonment of all seeking of Negro votes in the North . . . [in favor of] a new and triple alliance between the Midwest farm belt, the racists of the Old South and those political forces in the Northern suburbs that more and more seek to exclude Negroes from their neighborhoods and segregate them in old core cities."[5]

Under Goldwater's lead, that is precisely what happened. His harshly-worded conservatism and criticism of civil rights measures—he would be one of only eight non-Southern senators to vote against the 1964 Civil Rights Act—sent a clear signal of the party's new stance.[6] He captured the GOP nomination in 1964. But his bellicose position on dealing with the threat of communism and his racial extremism were distinctly unappealing to an electorate that two years earlier had been to the brink of nuclear war with the Soviet Union during the Cuban Missile Crisis and was still traumatized by the murder of its charismatic president just one year earlier. In the 1964 election, LBJ triumphed in a landslide. Goldwater won just six states— but five of them were the Southern states where resistance to the civil rights movement remained most entrenched— Mississippi, Alabama, South Carolina, Louisiana, and Georgia. Goldwater won those states by huge margins.[7]

Four years later, Nixon, once again the Republican candidate, adopted a more detailed Southern strategy, prompted in part by the impact the independent presidential campaign of Alabama's segregationist governor, George C. Wallace, was having on white Republican and disaffected Democratic voters. Wallace had dropped the crude racist language he used during the late 1950s and early 1960s. Instead, he used code words and phrases—such as "centralized government," "law and order," "pseudo-liberal," "individual rights," "radical feminism," and even "Harvard"—to stake out a position of resistance to liberalism that on the surface could not be said to be racist. As Thomas B. Edsall noted, "The roots of contemporary conservative rhetoric go directly back to the issue of race in the early 1960s. . . . [I]n political terms, racially coded rhetoric has served over the past four decades to bring together—to 'bundle'—and to unify key Republican messages."[8] From then on, Republican leaders did little more than rhetorically nod in the direction of the party's abolitionist roots—the more to enable its white base to convince itself it was not really part of a racist organization than out of any pro-civil-rights twinges. Black America observed, and voted accordingly. Where blacks had given 32 percent of their votes to Nixon in 1960, Goldwater got 6 percent in 1964, and four years later a victorious Nixon would get only 15 percent. In the nine presidential elections since 1968, only one Republican—Gerald R. Ford in 1976—would score that high.[9]

Nixon's disgrace over the Watergate scandal and the electorate's shock over the American defeat in Southeast Asia temporarily sidetracked the GOP's plan for national political success, as voters chose moderates—one Republican, Gerald R. Ford, and one Democrat, Jimmy Carter—whose bland demeanors they hoped would help heal the nation. But the Iran hostage crisis devoured the Carter administration and swung the 1980 election to Ronald Reagan.

Reagan's political record as a long-standing Goldwater ally—he, too, had opposed the 1964 Civil Rights Act—and a two-term governor of California left no doubt about his commitment to a far-right conservatism. But it still came as a shock when Reagan opened his general campaign in September 1980 with a speech at the Neshoba Counter Fair in Philadelphia, Mississippi—the site of the then-unsolved 1964 murders of three civil rights workers—extolling states' rights.

Using "extol" to describe Reagan's reference might at first appear misleading, given that he used it only once and seemingly almost in passing. The phrase was embedded in brief comments he made about federal government involvement in schools: "Programs like education and others should be turned back to the states and local communities with the tax sources to fund them," he said. "I believe in states' rights. I believe in people doing as much as they can at the community level and private level." Ever since, Reagan apologists have seized upon his brevity in using the phrase to declare that he's been unfairly tarnished. David Brooks, the *New York Times* conservative columnist, wrote in a November 2007 op-ed that to claim that Reagan had deliberately used the phrase to send a coded appeal to bigoted whites was a "slur . . . one of the most heinous charges imaginable. . . . It posits that there was a master conspiracy to play on the alleged Klan-like prejudices of American voters, when there is no evidence of that conspiracy." Brooks explained Reagan's decision to attend the Neshoba County Fair as merely one stop on the Reagan campaign trail. He noted that Reagan went from the fair to deliver a speech to the annual convention of the National Urban League, the civil rights organization, and, among other campaign-related duties, he visited the South Bronx, then the nation's stark symbol of urban decline, and met with the editors of the two Johnson Publishing Company magazines, *Ebony* and *Jet*, Black America's most influential publications. Brooks asserted that his activities in the week after the fair visit proved his words there were within the bounds of normal political campaigning. "You can look back on this history in many ways. It's callous, at least, to use the phrase 'states' rights' in any context in Philadelphia. Reagan could have done something wonderful if he'd mention civil rights at the fair. He didn't. And it's obviously true that race played a role in the GOP's ascent. Still, the agitprop version of this week—that Reagan opened his campaign with an appeal to racism—is a distortion."[10]

Lou Cannon, the former *Washington Post* White House reporter who's written several biographies of Reagan, supported Brooks's claims in a subsequent column in the *Times* nine days later. Cannon characterized the view that Reagan was making a racist appeal as untrue, a "myth" because, he wrote, "[f]irst, Ronald Reagan was not a racist." As proof, Cannon cited two incidents from the 1930s. When two black teammates on his college football team in Illinois were barred from a hotel where the team was staying, Reagan took them to his nearby hometown to spend the night with his family; and while a sports announcer in Iowa after college, Reagan apparently made clear his opposition to Major League Baseball's ban of black players.

Returning directly to the states' rights speech, Cannon added that "[f]ar from being a masterstroke, the Neshoba speech was a mistake made by a candidate who had not yet become the skilled operator the nation would see as president." Rather than winning Reagan more votes among Southern whites, Cannon wrote, the "Neshoba appearance hurt" Reagan with white moderate voters throughout the country "who wanted a president who would be sensitive to minority issues."[11]

The holes in both columns' defense of Reagan's racial politics were gaping.

Cannon's dependence on the two incidents from Reagan's young adulthood to prove an absence of both personal racial bigotry and racist practices and rhetoric had the opposite effect of emphasizing what both writers were omitting—everything from Reagan's clearly stated opposition to the 1964 Civil Rights Act to the voluminous anti-black statements and actions of his subsequent eight years in the White House. Further, it beggared credulity to pose, as both Brooks and Cannon did, the Ronald Reagan of 1980—by then his three decades of high-level political experience included governing California during the fractious 1960s and 1970s—as a political naïf who had somehow captured the Republican nomination without being committed to the GOP's dependence on the Southern strategy.

As many less biased observers have noted over the years, Neshoba County was hardly a traditional stop on the national political campaign trail—Reagan, prodded by one of the GOP's rising young southern representatives in Congress, Trent Lott, was the first presidential candidate to appear there. But its importance to the GOP as a sign of the effectiveness of its Southern strategy was clear. As political analyst Thomas F. Schaller noted, Neshoba County had been "suffering from a severe case of electoral schizophrenia" in the previous four presidential elections. In 1964 the electorate had given Goldwater 95 percent of its votes; in 1968 it had given 82 percent to the unsuccessful presidential bid of former Alabama governor George Wallace, the most prominent political racist in the country; and then in 1972 88 percent voted for Richard Nixon's re-election. However, in 1976, Georgia governor Jimmy Carter's winning campaign for the White House captured the majority vote of every southern state except Virginia— and by little more than thirty votes, the approval of Neshoba County voters, too. Carter's victory showed that, if they chose moderate southern candidates, the Democrats could disrupt the GOP's appeal in the region. That threat was why Neshoba County loomed large in the thinking of GOP strategists. Given its infamous history, in 1980 there was no better place to make the GOP candidate's position on race clear.[12]

True, Reagan spoke in code. But that's precisely the utility of coded appeals. They can be made briefly, even offhandedly, because their implicit meaning is always clear. Using the phrase "states' rights" to refer to federal oversight of the actions of southern state and local agencies, and doing so in the very community where a notorious civil-rights-related murder had occurred, leaves no room for doubt about its meaning, or Reagan's intent in using it.

Nonetheless, Reagan gained 12 percent of the black vote, bringing to the public's attention a small and, conservatives claimed, growing number who believed as he and other white conservatives did.

One black man to cast a vote for Reagan was Nathan Wright Jr., an educator, minister, and longtime civil rights activist who had been among the most prominent advocates of the concept of Black Power in the 1960s. In 1981 Wright said he was convinced that racism no longer had "a damn thing" to do with the predicament of Black America and that Reagan, a man of "principle and pragmatism," was committed to helping blacks advance. Another black Reagan supporter was Gloria E. A. Toote, a real estate entrepreneur in New York who, as a Howard University law student in the early 1950s, had conducted research for the team of civil rights lawyers arguing the *Brown v. Board of Education* cases. She said there were "many ideas that have been discussed within the administration which can be very meaningful to the black community. If blacks blindly reject anything proposed by Washington as anti-black, we'll hurt ourselves very seriously." A third to cast his vote for Reagan, scholar Thomas Sowell, of the Hoover Institution, a conservative think tank, declared that the black poor had been deeply hurt by the "political interventionist state" and by black civil rights leaders more interested in securing their own positions than aiding their less fortunate brethren. Yet another was Arthur Fletcher, who, as an assistant labor secretary in the Nixon administration, had implemented an effective affirmative action plan for the building-trades unions. Fletcher believed that the GOP under Reagan was "in a tremendous position to make inroads among the black electorate. The big question is," he continued, "are they going to do anything about it?"[13]

Each of these individuals, with long-standing ties to the Republican Party, asserted that a sizable number of blacks agreed with the bedrock conservative political beliefs of limited government, free-market enterprise, and individual self-reliance. Moreover, they thought the social programs begun or expanded during the Johnson presidency had failed and should be eliminated; they opposed affirmative action; and they favored massive government deregulation. Black America has always had a conservative element. But not until the beginning of the Reagan presidency had it been asserted with such vigor that, given just a little encouragement, a black conservative vote was available for the Republican Party to tap into.

In fact, Reagan's capturing 12 percent of the black vote, a figure that has been equaled or bettered by Republican presidential candidates in only three of the last eleven elections, did seem significant.[14] Given the anger that Reagan's "states' rights" speech had provoked just three months before the election, quite a number of black Americans were making the GOP a stunning offer: they were ready to be recruited.

A month after the election came another sign: several leading black and white conservatives, with the backing of Edwin Meese III, who would become a chief Reagan White House aide and eventually attorney general, convened a Black Alternatives Conference at the Fairmont

Hotel in San Francisco. Among those attending were several firmly in the conservative camp: Thomas Sowell; Milton Friedman, a University of Chicago professor and considered one of the gurus of the conservative movement; Walter E. Williams, a black George Mason University economist; and a young aide to Missouri senator John C. Danforth named Clarence Thomas. Among the progressives there were Percy E. Sutton, a former political officeholder in New York City who had developed a multimillion-dollar communications empire; economist Bernard E. Anderson of the University of Pennsylvania; and two political scientists: Martin L. Kilson of Harvard; and Charles V. Hamilton of Columbia, whose books included *Black Power: The Politics of Liberation in America*, published in 1968, which he co-wrote with Kwame Toure (then, Stokely Carmichael).

Hamilton's and Kilson's comments were instructive at the time of the conference and in hindsight. Hamilton took issue with several speakers' contention that black voters had become apathetic.

"The issue," Hamilton asserted, "regarding politics in the context of black alternatives for the 1980s is not a matter of party labels—Democratic, Republican . . . [nor of] ideological identification—liberals, conservatives, integrationists, nationalists. It is rather what I would call . . . the three Ps—process, product, and participation. . . . [W]hen the process is perceived as related to the products the people want, then participation will increase."[15]

When Kilson spoke, he pressed the point that what he called the "homogenized black leadership policy" that was prevalent in Black America had been valid through the early 1970s but had now outlived its usefulness. He believed that black Americans needed to "diversify" their political alliances and allegiances in order to respond to the "incredibly pressing need for policy spread, policy redefinition . . . [and] greater policy variation." In his words, "The left/liberal axis no longer has—if it ever did have—a monopoly on effective policy for black needs," and "there is too high a cost associated with black policy isolation from conservative initiatives in American political life." Kilson concluded that Black America needed to encourage the development of more "trans-ethnic black political leaders, both liberal and conservative, but especially the latter."[16]

There seemed to be significant reason to hope that the "policy spread" Kilson and Hamilton said they welcomed and blacks needed would come about. In part, the expansion of the black middle class had been well under way since the late 1960s. The rising bourgeoisie of white ethnic groups had always proved the political scientists and sociologists in academia right: many had shown themselves eager to shed their working-class-bred political allegiances to the Democratic Party for their new class interests as Republicans. One might have expected the same to happen with the new black middle class. Bernard Anderson, of the University of Pennsylvania, thought the new class of black business professionals then reaching significant numbers, many of them trained at the best business schools, would help drive that dynamic. "I'm not talking about [blacks in companies'] urban affairs or affirmative action posts," he said. "I'm talking about people in marketing, sales, production-management positions, people whose jobs involve the technical business functions. . . . This is fundamentally a new group among blacks." As support for his thesis, Anderson pointed out that the small audience at the Fairmont conference included a substantial number of these black professionals—an assistant treasurer at IBM, the chief account executive at one of California's major banks, a project manager for the giant Bechtel construction company, a senior vice president of another of California's major banks, and so on.[17] With this group as the vanguard of a conservative-oriented effort to mobilize Black America, it was just a matter of following Hamilton's advice about the "three Ps." Make the process inviting and the product appealing, and the participation—involvement in the conservative movement and voting for Republican candidates—would materialize.

But it didn't happen.

Instead, the Reagan White House quickly became the most anti-black administration since that of Woodrow Wilson sixty years earlier. Once in office, Reagan, among other things, cut the federal budget for civil rights enforcement; opposed passage of measures to end discrimination in housing; tried to undermine the Voting Rights Act; initially opposed naming a federal holiday for Martin Luther King Jr.; disparaged affirmative action and ordered the Justice Department to oppose plans requiring goals and timetables in hiring and promotion of white women and people of color; and expressed support for the apartheid regime in South Africa. In the latter controversy, when Congress passed a law approving sanctions against South Africa's government, Reagan vetoed it (Congress overrode the veto). In one of his more controversial actions, Reagan granted the fundamentalist Christian institution Bob Jones University the educational tax exemption routinely given colleges and universities, despite its racist policies that violated federal law. When a public outcry ensued, Reagan claimed the federal law regarding the school's policies was unclear. The Supreme Court found no such ambiguity when the case reached it. The justices unanimously ruled that the administration's action was invalid.

It's a long way from the expectations voiced during the Black Alternatives Conference a quarter century ago to today's 85-percent-plus levels of support given by blacks at the highest income levels to interventionist government policies in innumerable surveys and the Democratic Party in the voting booth. It's a long way from those expectations to black billionaire Bob Johnson's hard-line support for affirmative action.[18] The major reason why the "three Ps" relationship between blacks and the Republican Party—process, product, and participation—never worked is because the GOP, which had been expertly applying the three Ps strategy to the white middle and working classes, didn't want a substantial, involved black participation. It's as simple as that: the GOP didn't want black votes in 1980 and is no more willing to support black conservatism nearly thirty years later. Instead, the GOP's relationship with blacks is one of tokenism and window dressing.

Reagan and his successor, George H. W. Bush, employed that strategy—rhetorical expressions of goodwill here, a black appointment there, all masking hostile acts—with blunt force. Throughout his presidency, Reagan refused to meet with the heads of the National Urban League, the NAACP, and other members of the traditional civil rights groups. Instead, he met with groups that were handpicked by his staff. For example, in early 1985, on Martin Luther King Jr.'s birthday, the president, just past a sweeping reelection victory against Walter F. Mondale, met with a group of twenty conservative black business executives, educators, and heads of local organizations to hear their "agenda for black progress." Robert Woodson, the group's chairman, said that its purpose was "to establish a strategic alliance between the black community and the Reagan administration. . . . It's unproductive to stand outside and complain. Every time there is a news show, every time there is an issue, people go to [the traditional civil rights leaders]."[19] Shortly afterward, Reagan weighed in, telling reporters that the complaints of civil rights leaders that he would not meet with them had led him to "the conclusion that maybe some of those leaders are protecting some rather good positions that they have, and they can protect them better if they keep their constituency aggrieved and believing that they have a legitimate complaint. If they ever become aware of the opportunities that are improving," he added, "they might wonder whether they need some of those organizations."[20]

By that time, Reagan's charges had become the standard response of white and black conservatives to explain the overwhelming disapproval their message continued to generate among blacks. Put simply, they charged that civil rights leaders talked so much about racism in order to maintain their well-paying positions and their hold on the masses of black people. It was a response that intertwined two major elements of the racist canon. One was a revival of the old canard that Reconstruction had failed because the black politicians of that era were corrupt—and by extension, so are the black leaders of today who press issues of racism. The second implied complaint was that the black civil rights leadership was so powerful, it held the mass of blacks spellbound with harangues about racism. The other side of that coin, of course, is that the mass of blacks are too stupid to realize where their own best interests lie. In effect, this merely recycled the "few bad apples" or "outside agitator" gambit that segregationists in the South had clung to in the 1950s and early 1960s to explain why "their" Negroes were suddenly marching in the streets: they were being swayed by civil rights activists and too dumb to know what was good for them.

The outside-agitator charge in a slightly transformed guise continues to have enormous appeal, as evidenced by the zeal with which many people, from media columnists to bloggers, vehemently denounce the Reverends Jesse Jackson and Al Sharpton whenever any racial controversy arises, regardless of whether they're involved in the particular issue or not. The tactic—used today by blacks as well as whites—is most often a means for the critic to avoid grappling with the actual racial issues and actions at hand—just as it was for the segregationists of yesteryear. One revealing example of the gambit occurred in October 2007, when the *Washington Post* published a lengthy op-ed column of 1,381 words in which the writer declared Sharpton both "irrelevant" to a proper consideration of racial issues and "divisive" within the black community. This was the column's focus in spite of the fact that the writer acknowledged that an April 2007 *Wall Street Journal-*NBC News poll found that nearly 50 percent of blacks expressed a positive opinion of Sharpton.[21] A colleague of Sharpton's, in a letter to the *Post*, posed the obvious question: if Sharpton is so irrelevant, why did the writer devote so many words to him?

In the 1980s, the Reagan administration and black conservatives incessantly employed the tactic of claiming that the leaders of the traditional black civil rights groups were passé. But there was yet another layer to the cynical game the administration was playing on race. It was revealed by a news story in the *Washington Post* that appeared several days after Reagan met with Woodson's group of conservative black business executives. The article reported that several leading black Republican political operatives, including the chairman of the National Black Republican Council, were furious that the president had met with the Woodson group and not invited them to the meeting. The black politicos had taken their complaints to Vice President Bush, asserting that the president's staff was ignoring their policy suggestions and not funneling any political appointments or government business contracts their way. "White Republicans, even the boys in the White House, are making millions off the president," one of the sources for the story said. "They have no problem with connections when you are white, but if blacks try to get into the game, they say it's not fair, it's affirmative action." Another referred to Reagan's pledge in 1980 that his appointments to the White House staff would be color-blind, meaning black staffers would not be assigned to just "black" affairs. "It was a sham seduction," added this source, noting that there was only one black on Reagan's White House staff. "It effectively took all black influence out of the White House."[22] In other words, while the administration was using black Republican operatives to justify shunning black civil rights leaders, it was also playing one group of black conservatives against another.

The Southern strategy guidebook developed by the Reagan White House continued to bear fruit for his vice president and anointed successor. Despite the lift that the combination of Reagan's political success and the Democrats' decade-long malaise should have provided, George H. W. Bush was badly trailing Massachusetts governor Michael Dukakis, the Democratic candidate. That is, until campaign aides discovered that, during Dukakis's tenure, a man convicted of a murder committed during a robbery in the 1970s had kidnapped a white couple and raped the woman while on release from prison under the state's weekend furlough program. The man's name was William J. Horton. No one had ever called him "Willie" until Bush's no-holds-barred campaign guru, Lee Atwater, renamed him so that white voters would not miss the point. Bush, aided by Dukakis's ineffective response to the attempt to portray him as a robotic technocrat who was soft on crime, began to climb in the polls. Unlike Reagan, Bush had early in his political career been supportive of civil rights, in the fashion of moderate, eastern establishment Republicans. But the "Willie" Horton maneuver bore witness to the fact that, now that he was titular head of the party, he wouldn't shrink from playing conservative race politics. His political legacy to the country would be his appointment of Clarence Thomas to the U.S. Supreme Court. Thomas, while still a protégé of Senator John C. Danforth, one of the most respected Republicans in Washington, had found a secure niche in the 1980s as head of the Equal Employment Opportunity Commission. In 1990, Bush appointed Thomas, whose legal experience was meager and who had never argued a case in court, to the U.S. Court of Appeals in Washington, the second most prestigious court in the land. A year later, in 1991, Bush, describing Thomas as "the best qualified candidate," nominated him to the nation's highest court.[23]

Thomas's career advancement exemplified the cover provided to the GOP for its systematic anti-black politics by a few black Reagan and Bush appointees and black conservative intellectuals. They were the black faces that allowed white conservatives to use their rhetoric about color-blindness both as a weapon to enable them to oppose affirmative action and other public policies of particular importance to blacks and as a shield to escape accountability for the racial tokenism that has, in this era when American society has become more and more diverse, kept the GOP high command and its elected office-holding and convention-delegate ranks virtually all white. Indeed, it is as revealing as it is astonishing that during the past quarter century, when conservatism dominated the political discourse, and the Republican Party scored substantial electoral victories, only two black Republicans have served in Congress: Gary Franks of Connecticut, and J. C. Watts of Oklahoma. Further, according to figures compiled by the Joint Center for Political and Economic Studies, only fifty of the more than nine thousand black elected officials in the country are Republicans.[24]

There is a simple explanation for such a complete failure by a party that until November 2006 was justly celebrated for its long-term strategic political thinking and its tactical skill at winning elections: the Republican Party takes black Americans for granted. Typically it is said that the Democratic Party takes blacks for granted, and that assertion has been perpetuated for decades by the GOP leadership and by otherwise astute political analysts in the media. In fact, it shows how Orwellian the racial discourse in America sometimes becomes that this could happen: conventional wisdom declares that the one political party through which black Americans have gained a measure of political success and public-policy benefits is indifferent toward blacks. The other party, however, despite its atrocious lack of success in electing black candidates and devising policies that would lure black voters to vote for its white candidates, too, continually excuses its failure by saying that black voters just don't understand what it has to offer them. But the Republicans' skillful courtship of the Hispanic American electorate between 2000 and 2004, by which it increased its percentage of the Hispanic vote to 31 percent, proved that it understands very well how to woo new voting blocs. Just apply the fundamental rule of political campaigning: give the voters something to vote for.

That is what Republican National Committee chairman Ken Mehlman, standing before the NAACP national convention, as he had stood before other black organizations, was pledging to do. The skeptics were many, and they had added several controversies of recent years—including Senator Trent Lott's public pining for the days of Jim Crow—to the long list of GOP transgressions. Donna Brazile, a Democratic Party strategist, who had managed Al Gore's 2000 presidential campaign, said, "For black voters it is about deliverables. They want results, and if Ken and the GOP can deliver jobs, economic development, and access to good education and health care, he will bring home more black voters."

It was not to be. Mehlman's promise to the NAACP was made the month before Hurricane Katrina struck New Orleans on August 29, 2005. And his words were spoken before the Bush administration's response to the devastation of Hurricane Katrina seriously damaged its standing with whites and savaged it with blacks.

If the Bush administration's preparation for a storm such as Hurricane Katrina was atrocious, which it was; and its immediate response to the storm by the soon-to-be-ridiculed Michael Brown, director of the Federal Emergency Management Administration (FEMA), was inexcusably poor, which it was, then the administration's response to the political backlash that began to emerge on the first day of the storm was baffling. The entire world could see that the region, and especially New Orleans, had been overwhelmed and an extraordinary human tragedy was unfolding. Yet top White House officials behaved as if Katrina was a hurricane that had done relatively little damage. Bush reinforced this out-of-touch

attitude when he finally traveled to New Orleans and ut-
tered the infamous words praising Brown, his appointee
as FEMA head, whom he said was "doing a heckuva job."
For two days after the storm hit, Condoleezza Rice kept
up her vacation schedule in New York, where television
sound cameras filmed her shopping for shoes and attending a Broadway show. At the show, sound cameras caught
the marked catcalls and shouts of "What about New Orleans!" that followed Rice as she was introduced to the
audience before the curtain went up.[25] Of course, as secretary of state, it wasn't her responsibility to be involved
in responding to the hurricane. But her behavior nonetheless seemed cavalier and inappropriate for a woman
born in the South and occupying high political office in
an administration already drawing criticism for its con-
fused response to the crisis. It soon became apparent that
FEMA was a hallmark of the president's approach to
staffing federal agencies. They were parking places for
personal friends, friends of friends, and party or conservative movement apparatchiks, of which Brown was typical.
Hurricane Katrina served as a prime and tragic example
of what that can lead to.[26]

The American public learned several truths from Katrina. They noticed and were shocked by the multiple
failures of the local, state, and, most of all, federal government, and the rawness of black poverty that was exposed.
And they saw that the Bush administration's management skills were not what had been advertised by the

GOP platform and its spin doctors. The public had already discovered the depth of this false advertising when it came to administering the war in Iraq. Katrina made it abundantly evident that the administration could show stunning incompetence stemming from cronyism and inattention to duty in domestic crises as well. The polls of September and October 2005 offered stark testimony on the political impact of the storm. The Pew Research Center poll of early September found that 67 percent of Americans believed that Bush could have done more to improve the relief effort; only 28 percent thought his actions were acceptable. His overall job approval rating dropped to 40 percent, while the percentage of those who disapproved of his management climbed to 52 percent. For the first time since the terrorist attacks of September 11, a majority of Americans—56 percent—said the president should focus more on domestic issues than the war on terrorism, and they worried that the hurricane would cause an economic recession. This poll, and all others done during this period, also revealed sharp political and racial divides, with Democrats and Independents expressing far greater disapproval of Bush than Republicans, and blacks showing far more disapproval than whites.

In the Pew poll, 70 percent of blacks expressed anger over the government's response to Katrina, compared with 46 percent of whites, and 71 percent of blacks said the disaster indicated that racial inequality in America remained a major problem, while 56 percent of whites said that was

not a particularly important lesson of the calamity.[27] Just
one measure of the fury generated among black Americans by the government's botched response to Katrina is a
brief debate that broke out in the media over whether
Bush's approval rating among blacks had sunk to 2 percent, as an NBC News/*Wall Street Journal* poll estimated,
or whether that poll had not included enough blacks in
the survey to be valid. Most observers thought the latter,
insisting that Bush's approval rating among blacks was
closer to a range of 10 to 14 percent—a figure that
would still be unprecedented in polling history. David
Boisitis, a senior fellow at the Joint Center for Political
and Economic Studies, a Washington think tank that
tracks black American affairs, told the *Washington Post*
that he doubted the extremely low figure. "But would I be
surprised if it's 10 or 12?" he asked. "No," he said, adding
that in calculating approval ratings, 10 is "about as low as
you can go."[28]

Like all Americans and much of the world, blacks outside the devastated region were stunned by "the sheer
geographic extent of the calamity, covering 90,000 square
miles of Gulf coast, with floodwaters containing gasoline,
chemicals and human and animal waste, and a complete
meltdown of the region's communications networks."[29] In
addition, the depth of black poverty the hurricane exposed
in New Orleans and across the Gulf region was confirmed
by the U.S. Census Bureau, which in an extraordinary co-
incidence released its annual report on income, poverty,

and health insurance just days before the hurricane struck. The images of the hurricane powerfully underscored the reality behind the statistics.

The census report showed that, despite America's general economic recovery since 2001, the bottom had literally fallen out from under millions more Americans in the past 5 years: 4 million more Americans were living in poverty than before the economic recession of 2001, pushing the total up to 37 million Americans, and 4.6 million more Americans could no longer afford their health insurance, pushing that total figure to 45.8 million. As everybody knew, a disproportionate percentage of poor Americans were black: Katrina gave them names and faces for all of America—and the world—to see.

The import of these figures was underscored by a demographic profile the Associated Press published on September 4 of residents in the three dozen sections of Alabama, Mississippi, and Louisiana hit hardest by the storm. This area made up the Black Belt of the South, so called because it contained the greatest concentration of blacks during the centuries of slavery and the years of Jim Crow that followed until the black migrations of the twentieth century reduced the South's black population. The AP analysis, based on census data, determined that residents in these areas were predominantly people of color, still predominantly black, and were twice as likely to be poorer than the national average. Twenty percent of these areas' residents didn't own a car, compared to the national average of 10 percent. Nearly 25 percent of those who lived there had incomes below the poverty line, almost double the national average. One in a hundred households in these areas didn't have adequate plumbing—running hot and cold water, a shower or bath, and an indoor toilet—compared to the national average of one in every two hundred households. The indicators of poverty were even worse in particular neighborhoods in the cities of New Orleans; Pascagoula, Mississippi; and Mobile, Alabama.

The depth of such poverty did not surprise some observers. University of South Carolina historian Dan Carter told the AP that such figures shouldn't be surprising, adding that there's usually "not a lot of interest in [issues of poverty], except when there's something dramatic. By and large, the poor are simply out of sight, out of mind."[30] And Cornel West, the Princeton professor and philosopher, told the British newspaper *The Observer:* "It takes something as big as Hurricane Katrina and the misery we saw among the poor black people of New Orleans to get America to focus on race and poverty. It happens about once every thirty to forty years."[31] To be sure, many black Americans had a keener sense than most whites that considerable poverty still existed in America, particularly among blacks. But even for them, the visual depiction of desperate people trapped by the storm and the government's inaction, along with the vividness of the written dispatches, cast a particularly stark, brutal light on the statistics. The Pew survey had found that 43 percent of black

Americans (compared to 26 percent of white Americans) living outside the Gulf region had relatives or directly knew someone living there.[32] For this group, the plaintive appeal made to an AP reporter by a New Orleans resident who had been trapped at the city's convention center for five days was the sound of a voice they could hear. "Let them know," the man said, "we're not bums. We have houses. Our houses were destroyed. We have jobs. It's not our fault that we didn't have cars to leave."[33]

Katrina was revelatory in yet another way. There is a long history of politicians and political parties benefiting from a swift, smart, and decisive response to disaster. Roosevelt was never more popular than during World War II; George W. Bush's first term was drifting until 9/11 gave it focus, direction, and sympathy with the electorate. Katrina, then, while a disaster for the region, was also a political opportunity for a Republican administration, especially one that had always declared it was keen to woo Black America. It was the chance Mehlman's careful rhetorical approach could have seized upon to show black Americans that the administration's actions in a time of acute distress spoke as loudly as its words. The simple truth for Black America is that a majority of black Americans know someone who is trapped in poverty or directly dependent on government benefits and a responsive federal bureaucracy for his or her quality of life.

However, instead of benefitting the opportunity pre-
sented by Katrina's epic tragedy, from Ken Mehlman's
high-visibility campaign in Black America was thoroughly
undermined. The black conservatives went to ground. "I
think it will hurt," Alvin Williams, head of the Black
America's Political Action Committee (BAMPAC), a conservative group, said at the time. "There's a lingering per-
ception among African American voters," he went on,
"that the Republican Party is not interested in cultivating
their votes, especially now that Hurricane Katrina, race,
and the Republican Party have been injected into the discussion." Not surprisingly, Williams insisted that the administration's slow response was not racially driven.[34]

That kind of quiet response—or indifference—was consis-
tent with earlier responses by black conservatives to the
eruption of racial issues that cast the GOP in a bad light
with black voters. They fell silent in December 2002 when
Senator Trent Lott of Mississippi saluted Strom Thur-
mond and suggested that our country would have been
better off if the then-segregationist candidate had won the
presidency in 1948. They went to ground when the University of Michigan case was being decided by the Supreme Court—even after Colin Powell and Condoleezza
Rice had spoken in favor of affirmative action. They were
quiet when it came to light in early 2005 that Armstrong
Williams, a syndicated columnist and longtime black

Republican operative, had a secret $240,000 contract from the federal Department of Education to push the administration's No Child Left Behind Act in his columns and on his syndicated television show. Williams, who had worked for Strom Thurmond and was a close friend of Supreme Court Justice Clarence Thomas, at first offered the lame excuse that he sincerely believed in the law and would have pushed it anyway. But his syndicated column and program disappeared.[35] The revelation about Williams followed earlier examples of a deliberate Bush campaign to spin news favorable to the administration via planted reporters at press conferences and via video of government events sent to television stations by supposedly independent freelance news-gathering companies. For blacks, however, the Williams episode raised the question of whether there were more black conservatives on a Bush administration secret payroll.

It was no surprise, therefore, that in the aftermath of Hurricane Katrina, in the wake of the inept administration response and the silence of black Republican voices, the new GOP initiative that Ken Mehlman had so carefully crafted collapsed. He would resurrect it yet again in the winter of 2006, with a heavy emphasis on the candidacies of Blackwell in Ohio, Swann in Pennsylvania, and Steele in Maryland, and accompanied by the usual confident predictions of electoral breakthroughs. Syndicated columnist Clarence Page, impressed by the possibilities of a group of viable GOP black candidates, predicted "a future presidential matchup that, I guarantee you, is just as reliable as any other serious long-range political prediction. Here it is: Democratic senator Barack Obama vs. Republican governor J. Kenneth Blackwell of Ohio."

Blackwell's loss, and that of the other black Republican candidates, was good news for the Democratic candidates and for the Democratic Party as a whole. But in the larger sense, it continued the chain of bad news Black America has been getting from the Republican Party for nearly half a century. While blacks have charted remarkable gains within the Democratic Party—in both elective and appointive office—and influence in the senior-level party councils, blacks remain all but invisible in the party of the "Big Tent." That means that the potential represented by the black conservatives who surfaced in the wake of the Reagan revolution of 1980 to extend blacks' involvement in the Republican as well as Democratic Party, and thereby end their partial isolation in American politics, still lies fallow. And with it, black Americans' chance to realize their full political might, for the good of Black America as a whole.

5

BLACKER THAN WHO?

The Furious Debate over Black Identity

"ONE LAST THING," BARACK OBAMA SAID TO THE EDITORS of *Newsweek* magazine, as they wrapped up their questions for a lengthy interview that would appear in the July 16, 2007, issue.

> This is unprompted by a question, but it's prompted by the cut or the angle you guys are taking. I may be off base here. But the impulse I think may be to write a story that says Barack Obama represents a "postracial politics." That term I reject because it implies that somehow my campaign represents an easy shortcut to racial reconciliation. It's similar to the notion that if we're all color-blind

then somehow problems are solved. I just want to be very clear on this so that there's no confusion. . . . Solving our racial problems in this country will require concrete steps, significant investment. We're going to have a lot of work to do to overcome the long legacy of Jim Crow and slavery. It can't be purchased on the cheap. I am fundamentally optimistic about our capacity to do that. And I do assert that there's a core decency in the American people and in white Americans that makes me hopeful about our ability to deal with these issues. But these issues aren't just solved by electing a black president.

Obama went on to add,

I think there's a temptation to posit me in contrast to Jesse [Jackson] or [Al] Sharpton, and the thing I am constantly trying to explain is that I'm a direct outgrowth of the civil rights movement, that the values of the civil rights movement remain near and dear to my heart. To the extent that I speak a different language or take a different tone in addressing these issues is a consequence of me having benefited from those bloody struggles that folks previously had to go through. And so to suggest somehow that I'm pushing aside the past in favor of this Benetton future is wrong.[1]

That some black Americans would decide that Barack Obama—who has self-identified as a black American since he reached the age in late childhood when questions of identity come to the fore; who worked as a community organizer in an impoverished black neighborhood; who married a dark-brown black American woman; and who has long attended a church with a black minister and a predominantly black congregation—was not "black enough" or wasn't a "real" black American spoke volumes about how explosive the issue of racial identity, particularly black racial identity, remains in America. Overwhelmingly, the mainstream media framed the often frenzied discourse as one initiated and pushed almost solely by blacks. That's simply wrong: there was plenty of evidence from late November 2006 to the fall of 2007 (as this book was being written) indicating that whites, too, were obsessed with parsing every facet of Obama's complex racial heritage.

Nonetheless, it is true that black Americans' seemingly unending, racially driven reaction to Obama's candidacy, charted in mainstream media news stories and opinion columns, in the blogosphere, and on innumerable talk radio programs, was particularly pronounced. It uncovered an astonishing depth of passion about something—black identity—many thought had been settled years, if not decades, ago. The debate offered evidence that a substantial number of black Americans are deeply unsettled about their own racial identity and their relationship to other black Americans and the larger American society, and that they are driven to anxiety whenever they see other blacks expressing opinions or acting in ways that seem to contradict the conventional wisdom some blacks themselves hold about what constitutes "black" behavior. The debate can become profoundly intricate, because the questioning of one's racial credentials, so to speak, is a long-held tradition among black Americans. It grew out of the need to present a united front against the pervasive bigotry blacks faced from whites. Today, polls show conclusively that large majorities of blacks believe discrimination remains widespread, albeit often in subtler guise than in the past. So, in that sense, it's not surprising that a black figure like Barack Obama would provoke among blacks a range of emotions from honest curiosity to skepticism to outright opposition. Nonetheless, and more positively, the debate shows that the opinions among blacks on what defines black identity—that is, the views of what it means to be a black American—are being expressed in wildly multiplying ways.

This variety is no longer a matter of the split that surfaced a quarter century ago between a small cohort of Republican-leaning black social and political conservatives, on the one hand, and the large body of blacks who vote Democratic on the other. Instead, what the debate about Barack Obama's racial "authenticity" uncapped was a geyser of opinion about black identity and racial responsibility in a period filled with sharply contrasting sets of images and statistics. One set offers evidence of a substantial expansion of opportunity for black Americans. It encompasses a large number of black Americans who have risen from the working class to the middle or upper-middle class in one generation. In many demographic respects, these upwardly mobile blacks mirror their counterparts among white Americans. However, the other set of images and statistics sounds an alarm about a cohort of black Americans ensnared in a tangle of problems—some structural, some of their own making—whose severity seems unabated.

The stew of ideas, attitudes, and biases is focused on Obama because his personal story represents in spectacular fashion the progress made by black Americans—and because his family experience has drawn out the variety of what black Americans think about who black Americans are.

This was a discussion within Black America that was waiting to explode. It began to bubble up in the fall of 2006 even before the midterm elections as the certainty of a sizable Democratic national victory drastically accelerated the Obama-as-presidential-candidate speculation. It's important to note that the sense of anticipation about his candidacy's racial meaning wasn't limited to blacks and white progressives. Even some conservative columnists said they would welcome it. Charles Krauthammer urged Obama to pursue the nomination, even though he declared himself certain that Obama would lose this time around to Hillary Clinton. In a column published ten days before the 2006 midterm elections, Krauthammer wrote, "When, just a week ago, Barack Obama showed a bit of ankle and declared the mere possibility of his running for the presidency, the chattering classes swooned. Now that every columnist in the country has given him advice, here's mine: He should run in '08. He will lose in '08. And the loss will put him irrevocably on a path to the presidency."

Krauthammer argued that the very thing which helped make Obama attractive as a candidate—his newness as a national figure—was also a drawback because, in the midst of the American war in Iraq and Afghanistan, American voters "will simply not elect a novice in wartime." But he said Obama's pursuit of the nomination would "cure his problem of inexperience" and make him "the presumptive front-runner in the next presidential election cycle."

Krauthammer also said that an Obama candidacy would benefit America in racial terms because "the country hungers for a black president. Not all of the country. But enough that, on balance, race would be an asset." Krauthammer referred to the similar fervor in the mid-1990s that produced "a loud national chorus" urging Colin Powell to run for the presidency. "Race is only one element in their popularity, but an important one," Krauthammer continued. "A historic one." A black candidate gaining the White House "would be an event of profound significance, a great milestone in the unfolding story of African Americans achieving their rightful, long-delayed place in American life."[2]

Krauthammer's comment that a viable black presidential candidate would be good for all of America is instructive. Any black candidate running a mainstream campaign—a Colin Powell, a Barack Obama, a black woman politician (when that moment comes)*—for the highest office in the land, the one all Americans vote for, would have provoked a response similar in scope and passion to that which greeted Obama's pursuit. And that's because it would mean that a black person would stand, not as a "black leader" or the black officeholder of a high political office, but as *the leader* of the United States of America, holding all of the powers and responsibilities of that office.

The frenzy provoked by Obama's candidacy suggests that the reality of a black president of the United States would require enormous adjustments on the part of many Americans in racial attitudes and in the pursuit of goals that are both race-related and seemingly unrelated to race. Many Americans, including black Americans, are by now used to seeing black men and women in positions of significant authority. But the totality of that imagined portrait—a black man and a black woman and a black First Family in the White House—is still a strikingly unusual vision. Barack Obama represented the possibility that, for the first time in American history, that vision could actually be at hand.

As Krauthammer's column indicated, that vision for many whites, not all of them in Obama's camp, was worth contemplating. They understood that in the larger sense

---

*I do not forget the 1972 campaign waged by Brooklyn congresswoman Shirley Chisholm for the Democratic nomination, which was won by South Dakota senator George McGovern. Chisholm's campaign, as important as it was, was that of an outsider.

the nation needs to accelerate its processes of assimilating its multiracial, multicolored population in ways that further the expansion of opportunity and break down the stereotypes of what positions are available to what kinds of people. America must figure out how to manage the new reality, one in which all individuals and groups are simultaneously asserting their claim to a share of the nation's bounty.

That includes women, white and otherwise. Indeed, despite the rhetoric disparaging the "old" Clintons, Hillary Clinton's campaign to be the first woman president was, from the beginning, equally invested with the possibility of constructing a new vision of what it means to be an American. For this country, having a "Madame President" would be a radical departure from the past. That is the reason explaining much of the fervor both for her and against her among white women. (Polls have consistently shown that Clinton's support among black women is higher in percentage terms than among white women.) The Clinton campaign is part of the debate among women as a whole, and white women in particular, about their identity in the first decade of the twenty-first century.

It was not surprising, however, that the debate about Obama's racial credentials took precedence in the mainstream media and the blogosphere. Obama was the newer face in the game. In addition, it soon became apparent that some blacks were eager to assert that, in their view, Obama was not really a black American.

Columnist Stanley Crouch, writing four days before the 2006 midterm elections, bluntly asserted, "Other than color, Obama did not—does not—share a heritage with the majority of black Americans who are descendants of plantation slaves." Referring to Obama's book *The Audacity of Hope,* Crouch said, "Obama makes it clear that, while he has experienced some light versions of typical racial stereotypes, he cannot claim those problems as his own—nor has he lived the life of a black American."

Crouch, who implied that he was descended from plantation slaves, left much unexplained. He did not specify what the importance of a black American being descended—or not—from a plantation slave means in our present time; nor whether he would consider a black American who was descended from the small number of pre-Civil War blacks who had never been enslaved—the so-called free blacks—a "real" black American. Nor did Crouch acknowledge that many blacks who are descendants of plantation slaves are also descendants of whites. Finally, Crouch didn't discuss what constituted "light versions of typical racial stereotypes" and whether experiencing only such bias would also disqualify a plantation-descended black American. Instead, Crouch went on to seemingly contradict himself by saying, "Of course, the idea that one would be a better or a worse representative of black Americans depending upon his or her culture or ethnic group is clearly absurd." In the end, however, he made his position clear: "[W]hen black Americans refer to Obama as 'one of us,' I do not know what they are talking about."³

In late January 2007, author Debra J. Dickerson wrote a highly controversial column for Salon.com that tracked along the same lines. Her purpose, she wrote, was "to point out the obvious: Obama isn't black."

Dickerson contended that because Obama was born of a Kenyan father from East Africa and a white American mother, he was not descended from the West Africans brought to America's shores as slaves in the colonial and antebellum eras. Rather, she said, Obama was like the "voluntary immigrants of African descent" who have come to America recently "with markedly different outlooks on the role of race in their lives and in politics." She continued: "At a minimum, it can't be assumed that a Nigerian cabdriver and a third-generation Harlemite have more in common than the fact that a cop won't bother to make the distinction. They're both 'black' as a matter of skin color and DNA, but only the Harlemite, for better or worse, is politically and culturally black, as we use the term."

Like Crouch, Dickerson narrowed her definition of a "real" black American to those descended from blacks held in bondage during the colonial and antebellum eras. She didn't acknowledge that the forced and consensual sexual coupling that occurred during slavery and ever since has made black Americans a highly mixed group.

Most black Americans are not only descended from West Africans; they are also descended from whites, American Indians, and to a lesser extent, from Latinos and Asian Americans as well. In her zeal to cast Obama as not truly a black American, Dickerson continually referred to his modern-day African roots, claiming at one point: "Not descended from West African slaves brought to America, he steps into the benefits of black progress (like Harvard Law School) without having borne any of the burden, and he gives white folks plausible deniability of their unwillingness to embrace blacks in public life. None of Obama's doing, of course, but nonetheless a niggling sort of freebie." Later, she returned to the two themes, asserting that whites are "swooning over nice, safe Obama" because they aren't "embracing a black man, a descendant of slaves. [They're] replacing a black man with an immigrant of recent African descent of whom [whites] can approve without feeling either guilty or frightened. . . . Even if Obama invokes slavery and Jim Crow, he does so as one who stands outside, one who emotes but still merely informs. . . . He signals to whites that the racial turmoil and stalemate of the last generation are past and that with him comes a new day in politics when whites needn't hold back for fear of being thought racist."[4]

Dickerson's is a curious argument, and not merely for the holes in her reasoning—such as her insistence on casting Obama as an immigrant because of his father (with whom he had very little contact throughout his life), when, like his mother, he was born an American. All but declaring that a full understanding of American blackness is genetically determined, Dickerson asserts that Obama can never really feel what it's like to be black because, by virtue of his father and his being raised by his white mother and grandparents, he didn't have a real black experience as a child and adolescent.

Dickerson had one kind of a black experience. She grew up in a hardscrabble neighborhood in St. Louis, Missouri, the daughter of former sharecroppers. After several rough missteps, she found a sense of ambition and discipline by enlisting in the U.S. Air Force, a choice that subsequently propelled her through three institutions of higher learning—including, like Obama, Harvard Law School. Perhaps that is the source of her declaring that Obama has enjoyed the benefits of black progress without having borne the burdens of being black. Nevertheless, it is strange that Dickerson would be so rigid in judging Obama's blackness qualifications. Her two books—an autobiography, *An American Story,* and *The End of Blackness: Returning the Souls of Black Folk to Their Rightful Owners*—are paeans to the right of black Americans to live as individuals free from what she scathingly denounces as the attempts of black "gatekeepers" to impose a stifling, uniform black ideology. It is those blacks, Dickerson writes in *The End of Blackness,* "who critique other blacks' choices—from styles of dress, to relationship partners, to careers, to political affiliation . . . who tell other blacks what they must think . . . who try to control the political, intellectual, and social discourse of other blacks," who are undermining black progress.[5]

Equally intriguing is the fact that, for all of Dickerson's categorical rejection of Obama for membership in Black America because of his mixed parentage, she herself is married to a white man by whom she has two biracial children. Shortly after she penned the column about Obama, she wrote one in which she expressed a great deal more sensitivity and understanding that her children would ultimately have to decide their relationship to the different parts of their racial heritage for themselves. But the column also revealed her decidedly ambiguous attitudes toward black Americans. Although she and her family live in a predominantly white community in upstate New York, and she worries that her children won't become acquainted with many aspects of black American culture, she refuses to expose them to any—be it soul food or visits to predominantly black churches. She explains: "I don't want to force experiences on my son and daughter just to make them feel black. . . . [W]e encounter very few black people and even fewer who are not mainstream professionals, with all the requisite class implications that follow (affluent, private-school educated, i.e., not very culturally black)."[6] That a black woman, an alumna of Harvard Law School, living an upper-middle-class existence with a white husband, would denigrate other middle-class blacks as insufficiently black offers a piercing comment on Dickerson's blacker-than-thou attitude toward Obama—and on how unsettled the issue of black identity is among some blacks.

More than four hundred readers blogged responses to Dickerson's column on Obama. Among the keenest responses was one that read:

> Regardless of Obama's ethnic background, he is a black man living in America. That's the way he's seen by pretty much all the non-blacks living in America, regardless of his Kenyan/white heritage. . . . True, a recent immigrant from Mali (or Jamaica or Suriname or wherever) who sells scented oils on 125th Street has a wildly different view of America, and different expectations of it, than the great-grandchild of Alabama cotton-picking sharecroppers—that goes without saying. But the fact remains that to the average white, Asian, or Latino American who meets him, he's just a black man—with all the stereotypes, good and bad, that that implies. . . . [H]e's essentially, still, just a black man (and I don't mean "just" in the diminishing sense, but in the sense that he's not seen as belonging to any other ethnic group. . . . We, the descendants of West African slaves, have now been in this country for so long . . . and spread out so much demographically and economically that our concerns have become far too variegated to be lumped together under one roof. And we're all, still, "really" black.[7]

Some observers lamented that the discussion was occurring at all, labeling it a sign of weakness among blacks (as if blacks were the only ones involved in the discussion) and a distraction from the efforts to solve blacks' problems. But such critics misunderstood a fundamental point about black Americans' existence over the last century: they've never stopped debating what it means to be a black American.

"How does it feel to be a problem?" That was the question posed by W. E. B. Du Bois in his classic 1903 book, *The Souls of Black Folk*. The book was published less than a decade after the 1896 Supreme Court decision in the *Plessy* case had declared that racial segregation was legal, stamping its imprimatur on the burgeoning laws and customs confining black Americans to a small corner of American life, and essentially stripping them in ways large and picayune of their status as American citizens. One subsequent battle of the Jim Crow era was to persuade white newspapers to capitalize the appellation "Negro" and to use the honorific "Mr.," "Mrs.," and "Miss" when referring in print to black adults. *Plessy* forced blacks, once again, to try to protect their identity as human beings, an identity that had always been under threat in America. For the first 250 years of white settlement in America, from the importation of the first Africans as slaves at Jamestown, Virginia, to the end of the Civil War in 1865, 80 to 90 percent of black Americans were identified in law and custom as "slaves." Increasingly, over time, they were also arbitrarily deprived of their African names and given English or sometimes Latin first names by those who enslaved them. It was the enslaved black Americans, not the tiny legion of free blacks, who were written into the Constitution in the "three-fifths clause" in 1787 in order to settle the dispute over the political power the slaveholding states would have in the new union. (The Constitution also excluded Hispanics, Asians, and American Indians from citizenship.) Not until the end of the Civil War could the scattered and broken black American community begin to piece together an integrated identity for itself. With *Plessy*, blacks' ability to build a coherent, self-respecting black identity was once again jeopardized.

Du Bois, with his unusual background and extraordinary achievements, was profoundly sensitive to how *Plessy* threatened blacks not only materially but psychologically. Born of Dutch, French Hugenot, and African stock, and raised in western Massachusetts just after the Civil War, Du Bois was educated at Fisk University, a black college, earned a second bachelor's degree at Harvard, conducted graduate studies at the University of Heidelberg, and completed a doctorate in history at Harvard (his thesis inaugurated the Harvard Historical Series). Du Bois possessed a fierce natural intelligence that made him one of the most brilliant men of his era, and yet, in spite of his impressive character and achievements, there would be no professorship at Harvard or any white college for him, no opportunities at all in the larger society.

Du Bois understood what white Americans' mistreatment and disregard meant for blacks. It meant they had to doubt themselves; they had to see themselves as a "problem." This was, he wrote, "a strange experience—peculiar even for one who has never been anything else."[8] Blacks' mistreatment by their fellow Americans had forced the Negro to be

born with a veil and gifted with second-sight in this American world—a world which yields him no true self-consciousness, but only lets him see himself through the revelation of the other world. It is a peculiar sensation, this double-consciousness, this sense of always looking at one's self through the eyes of others, of measuring one's soul by the tape of a world that looks on in amused contempt and pity. One ever feels his twoness—an American, a Negro; two souls; two thoughts, two unreconciled strivings; two warring ideals in one dark body, whose dogged strength alone keeps it from being torn asunder. This history of the American Negro is the history of this strife.[9]

Du Bois saw, forty years after the Civil War, that black Americans remained trapped in the grinding tension between the two American traditions: inclusion and exclusion. Both traditions had animated the American spirit from the colonies' very beginning. Both traditions were written into the Constitution of 1787—the words proclaiming self-evident truths of the inalienable rights of man hovering just a few paragraphs away from the three-fifths clause. Both traditions were in play at the turn of the twentieth century, too, when the flowery rhetoric of America as the world's "melting pot" democracy coexisted uncomfortably with the *Plessy* decision and a fierce bigotry against white ethnic immigrants from Catholic Ireland and southern and eastern Europe.

For all the Columbus Day parades celebrating that white ethnic floodtide, the widespread sentiment held by Americans of white Anglo-Saxon Protestant stock was expressed by the great Anglo-American novelist Henry James. His wealthy family had lived in lower Manhattan during the mid-nineteenth century when WASPs still held overwhelming sway in New York City and the country at large. In 1904, having returned to America from Europe for the first time in a quarter century, James was appalled as he surveyed Manhattan's teeming, polyglot environment. Following a brief trip to Ellis Island, the immigration center in New York Harbor, James wrote:

I think indeed that the simplest account of the action of Ellis Island on the spirit of any sensitive citizen [is that he] comes back from his visit not at all the same person that he went. . . . He had thought he knew before, thought he had a sense of the degree to which it is his American fate to share the sanctity of his American consciousness, the intimacy of his American patriotism, with the inconceivable alien; but the truth had never come home to him with any such force. In the lurid light projected upon it by those courts of dismay, it shakes him . . . to the depths of his being. . . . Let not the unwary, therefore, visit Ellis Island.[10]

Considering that James was heralded for his sympathetic and deft exploration of his characters' internal states beneath their outward garb, demeanor, and status, his view of the "new" Americans of his day is chilling evidence of how dominant the tradition of exclusion was at the time. That ideology was directed against white women and Americans of color, and, most of all, against blacks.

Du Bois understood that for blacks there was only one hope of solving the crisis they faced. They would have to not merely act, but *think* their way out. That meant, above all, that blacks had to consider whether the white racist ideology was right: were blacks inferior? The black masses' migration from the South initiated a long period of group introspection by exposing millions of blacks to the vibrant, raucous, modern, and freer urban North and by giving blacks some—but not all—of the tools to compete for a place in it. The severe discrimination they faced in the North (and urban South) also meant that their alleged inferiority would remain an open question. It could only be vanquished through achievement, by carving out a place of comfort and opportunity in American society despite the barriers they faced. Blacks' success in doing just this from the 1920s to the 1950s enabled them to expand Du Bois's definition of double-consciousness. At first, it had been a tool for self-diagnosis and questioning their own capabilities. Soon, however, they found that this "second sight" helped them navigate the discordant, wrenching paths of a modernizing America and partially shielded them from white supremacy's harsh demands for surrender. And as they grappled with the challenges of a world war, a stunning cultural renaissance, a devastating Great Depression, and, finally, a second war "to make the world safe for democracy," black Americans discovered they could use double-consciousness to examine White America, too. In other words, Black America refashioned double-consciousness from a burden into a compass and a gyroscope that they used to steady themselves and plot their course as they endured the seventy-year trek from *Plessy* to the civil rights victories of the mid-1960s.

No document more dramatically confirmed the results of that journey than the special issue that *Ebony* magazine, Black America's secular bible, published in August 1965. The cover article proclaimed its point by showing a stark white cutout of a man set against a black background and accompanied by the following headline: "The White Problem in America."

In a lengthy "Publisher's Statement," John H. Johnson, the founder of *Ebony* and, at that time, the most powerful black businessman in America, was blunt. "In the entire history of the period during which the area of the North American continent now known as the United States has been occupied by white Europeans and their descendants, the white man has been trying to explain away the Negro." Johnson spent half of his manifesto summarizing America's racial history, from the landing in Jamestown in 1619 of the first Africans brought as slaves to the Supreme Court's 1954 decision in the landmark *Brown* school desegregation case, repeating the refrain that whites had tried to "explain away" the denial of civil rights to blacks. He then went on to declare that the time for that was over:

> [T]he Negro in the pulpits, in the streets, in the schools, at the polls, in the halls of justice and in the legislative bodies of the land has emphasized that today he has earned his humanity and his full rights as a citizen. What has held him up? The unthinking white man—Mr. Charlie, Whitey, The Man—the unthinking white man who is the symbol to Negroes of all those whites who have "stood in doorways" to keep the Negro back.

Johnson concluded by writing,

> This brings us to this special issue, "The White Problem in America," and its reason for being. For more than a decade through books, magazines, newspapers, TV and radio, the white man has been trying to solve the race problem through studying the Negro. We feel that the answer lies in a more thorough study of the man who created the problem. In this issue, we, as Negroes, look at the white man today with the hope that our effort will tempt him to look at himself more thoroughly. With a better understanding of himself, we trust that he may then understand us better— and the nation's most vital problem can then be solved.[11]

Ebony, founded in Chicago in the mid-1940s, was condemned by some blacks and chided by others for being a relentlessly upbeat chronicler of black Americans' striving for middle-class status. But in that era when public school curricula discussed Negro slavery and Jim Crow in the sketchiest of terms, while virtually completely ignoring contributions made by blacks to American society, and when most white colleges and universities studied blacks only as a "problem people," *Ebony* was also a relentless popularizer of black history and Black America's most trusted source of news and analysis about the progress of the civil rights movement. There was nothing else like it. The magazine fully reflected the overwhelmingly majority sentiment of Black America—its steadfast but patient determination in the 1950s and early 1960s to secure full citizenship through reformist, civil means; and, by the mid-1960s, its increasingly bold social and political consciousness. Thus, Johnson's unequivocal demand in the magazine's August 1965 issue was proof that Black America's double-consciousness had traveled far from its beginnings as a tool of tentative self-analysis. It had become a fount of assertiveness, out of which poured all of the brash activism and rhetoric and style of the Black Power movement and the black cultural revolution of the late 1960s: the huge Afro hairdos, the African-inspired garb, the intricate Black Power handshakes and lingo, and even the overt or implicit messages of numerous rhythm and blues songs of the period. When James Brown, the "Godfather of Soul," hollered, "Say It Loud, I'm Black and I'm

Proud!" in the tumultuous year of 1968, everyone knew what that meant. And Black America was proud.

And yet, amid the ratcheting up of a militant black consciousness, some blacks objected to the new terms of identification. They opposed efforts to bar the use of "Negro"—which H. Rap Brown, then the chairman of the militant Student Nonviolent Coordinating Committee, called "a slave word"—in favor of "black," "Afro-American," and "African American."[12] Later, in the 1980s, the decade framed by Reagan-style conservatism on the one hand, and Reverend Jesse Jackson's two insurgent campaigns for the Democratic nomination on the other, a new black-identity debate broke out when many blacks wanted to eliminate "black" in favor of just "African American."

"To be called African American," Jackson said at a December 1988 news conference, "has cultural integrity. It puts us in our proper context. Every ethnic group in this country has a reference to some land base, some historical cultural base. African Americans have hit that level of cultural maturity."[13] Jackson's support for the name change undoubtedly helped stoke the resulting controversy, and references to it in the media and elsewhere have made it appear as if Jackson himself had arbitrarily pushed the matter. In truth, standing alongside Jackson at the news conference that day were people representing a broad spectrum of black political thought. They included Richard G. Hatcher, the former mayor of Gary, Indiana; Gloria E. A. Toote, a former Nixon administration official and a staunch supporter of Ronald Reagan; and officials from the National

Black Republican Council, the National Association of Black County Officials, and the NAACP. Indeed, the term "African American" was already in wide use throughout colleges and universities, school systems, and black radio stations. A subsequent *New York Times* article found substantial support for the name change. Written by Roger Wilkins, then a fellow at a Washington think tank and now a distinguished professor at George Mason University (and nephew of Roy Wilkins, the former NAACP leader), the article read: "Whenever I go to Africa, I feel like a person with a legitimate place to stand on this earth. This is a name for all the feelings I've had all these years."

Not all blacks agreed, however. A letter writer to the *Chicago Sun-Times* complained, "When did they take a vote on what blacks wanted to be called? They must have done it when I was asleep. Jesse Jackson and other black leaders have a lot of nerve speaking for all blacks."[14]

As with the controversy surrounding Barack Obama's racial heritage, some critics claimed that the proposal for a new "official" name was a distraction. But such dismissals miss the point about the debate over black identity—why it has always simmered within Black America, and why it comes to a boil at particular moments. The answer becomes evident when considering that the debates over black identity in the late 1960s and the 1980s occurred after blacks' civil rights had been won but when the question about their status in society was unusually contentious.

During both periods, the goal of blacks' assertiveness wasn't separation from but greater assimilation into American society. Pride in being black wasn't a weapon wielded against the American ideal, but rather black Americans' means of redeeming their past and altering the terms of the American tradition of inclusion to enable them to fit in. For three centuries, white supremacy had asserted that being black and American was a contradiction. Now that blacks had gained full legal rights, they were not going to make their blackness invisible. They were intent on declaring that they were black and American, too.

Further, the racist resistance to blacks' inclusion—the American tradition of exclusion—was sharply diminished. But as the rhetoric and actions of the Reagan and first Bush administrations underscored, it had not disappeared. Instead, it had adapted, fighting rearguard battles in various arenas bolstered by the Republican Party's adoption of coded racist appeals to whites. Finally, the advances charted by Black America have constituted only a partial victory—one reason for blacks' continued strong support for affirmative action. Coexisting with visible markers of progress are visible markers of crisis: a sizable black middle class versus a skyrocketing rate of incarceration of black males and the poor academic performance of a sizable percentage of black school pupils. Psychically, this was and remains a juxtaposition fraught with tension. Which portrait represents the real Black America? If a sizable number of black Americans can be successful, why are so many others mired in poverty and beset by a host of other social problems?

Who or what is to blame for those blacks at the bottom of the socioeconomic ladder? Has the political and social liberalism that carried Black America through the Jim Crow years to victory in the 1960s outlived its usefulness? Should we adopt new ways of thinking about reducing black poverty?

President George H. W. Bush's nomination of Clarence Thomas to the U.S. Supreme Court in 1991 brought these issues to a full boil. Not only was Thomas a protégé of two Republican presidents who had indulged in blatantly racist appeals and actions, but his views on key racial issues were diametrically opposite those of Justice Thurgood Marshall, the revered civil rights icon he was to replace. Thomas's nomination was deeply controversial from the outset, but the controversy was propelled to volcanic proportions when Anita Hill accused him of sexual harassment. His boosters argued that Thomas could not be turned away just because of his conservative views because he represented the new diversity of thought growing in post-civil-rights Black America—the very freedom to think as one wished that the civil rights movement had favored. And they won the day against his progressive and liberal opponents in the U.S. Senate (barely) and in Black America. Polls showed that a clear majority of blacks supported Thomas for the Court. (Support for Thomas in Black America has since plummeted to a percentage in the low 30s. Blacks' support for black political conservatism is far lower, as the paltry black vote totals for Republican presidential candidates shows.)

In other words, the initial controversy among blacks about Clarence Thomas's nomination was rooted in an examination of what the boundaries were of black identity that were right for the time. That issue—what black identity works best now—has always been at the heart of the debate over black identity; and since the civil rights victories in the 1960s, the debate has always been most intense when blacks have achieved notable successes but substantial problems persist, a juxtaposition suggesting that blacks' status in American society is still not secure.

In that regard, as Barack Obama's campaign for the Democratic presidential nomination was being celebrated as indicative of the country's expansive racial climate, it wasn't surprising that the largest civil rights demonstration America had seen since the mid-1960s was taking shape.

In late September 2007, more than 30,000 demonstrators, most but not all of them black, flooded the predominantly white, northern-Louisiana hamlet of Jena to protest the treatment of six black high school students who in December 2006 had been charged as adults with attempted murder for attacking a white fellow student. The attack was the culmination of a series of racially charged events at the high school that had begun the previous summer when several white students hung three nooses on the branches of the only shade tree on school grounds to mark it as a whites-only area. The students subsequently claimed not to know that the nooses symbolized

the lynching frenzy southern blacks endured during the
Jim Crow years. The protests of black students and their
parents in the fall of 2006 were rebuffed by the Jena school
board and police and prosecutor. That the student who
had been attacked spent only a few hours at a local hospi-
tal before attending a high school event that same evening
belied the alleged seriousness of his injuries, and the seriousness of the charges themselves.

The situation facing the Jena Six, as the black students
came to be called, was transmitted across the country
during a months-long grassroots campaign by black radio
announcers and students at historically black colleges and
universities in the South, and it galvanized Black America.* For many, the story was a familiar replaying of the
exercise of white racist privilege and "Southern justice"
blacks had long endured during the Jim Crow years;
many news accounts framed the story in civil-rights-
period terms. Another cause for the protestors' outrage
over the miscarriage of justice was their belief—and that
of Black America—that today's criminal justice system is

---

*The charges were reduced in the summer to second-degree bat-
tery before all but one of the students had gone to trial. That student, who had been kept in jail since his arrest because of a prior
conviction, was tried and, after a cursory defense by his lawyer,
swiftly convicted by an all-white jury of the new charge. However,
a federal appeals court reversed that conviction shortly before the
march occurred.

often unfair to black people, not just in Jena but every-where. The outlines of the case were familiar to many blacks, who have seen black males and, increasingly, black females become easy targets for schools to deliver dispro-portionate suspensions and expulsions, and for police of-ficers and prosecutors to arrest and jail.

That school disciplinary action and police and prose-cutorial action often work in tandem was underlined by an article published in the *Chicago Tribune* in late Sep-tember 2007, just days after the Jena demonstration. The article stated that data from the federal Department of Education and several scholarly longitudinal studies showed that black elementary and secondary students en-dure school suspensions and expulsions at dramatically disproportionate rates. The newspaper said that its own analysis of the federal data revealed that overall, black students are suspended and expelled at three times the rate of their white counterparts, and that in many states, the rate is far higher.

The news article went on to say that, contrary to the conventional wisdom, numerous research studies have shown that blacks' greater likelihood of growing up in poor families fails to explain the discipline disparity. "There simply isn't any support for the notion that . . . African American kids act out to a greater degree than other kids," commented Russell Skiba, a professor of educational psy-chology at Indiana University and a nationally recognized authority on school discipline. "In fact, data indicate that

African American students are punished more severely for the same offense, so clearly, something else is going on. We can call it structural inequity or we can call it institutional racism." Skiba and other experts on school discipline who were interviewed for the article said that black students' greater rates of suspension and expulsion, in addition to damaging the possibility that they will finish school, often lead to negative involvement with the criminal justice system. The article pointed out: "A history of school suspensions or expulsions is a strong predictor of future trouble with the law—and the first step on what civil rights leaders have described as a 'school-to-prison pipeline' for black youths, who represent 16 percent of U.S. adolescents but 38 percent of those incarcerated in youth prisons."[15]

The contrasting images of the status of black Americans could not be sharper. On the one hand, a black man, achieving at the highest levels of society, is seeking the highest office in the land. On the other, one dramatic incident followed by a federal statistics-laden document showing that many black youth are facing a systemic double jeopardy—from the push-out dynamic of the schools they attend and from a criminal justice system that expects to enroll them soon after they've been pushed out.

Adding to the current tension over black identity is an insidious and widespread practice among blacks and whites: using the foibles, flaws, and sins of any individual black person or small group of black people to generalize about blacks as a whole while not referring to blacks' accomplishments in the same way. The difference between using negative ethnically referenced generalizations and failing to use positive generalizations is especially striking in commentary about so-called gangsta rappers. Vulgar and buffoonish, gangsta rappers aren't a "black problem" but the most visible example of society's increasing use of ever more outrageous sexual titillation for cheap, momentary thrills and help in driving its frenetic conspicuous consumption. These performers belong in the same tawdry clique as shock jocks Opie and Anthony and Howard Stern, who use profanity and sophomoric sexual play while posing as societal outlaws. Black America is criticized because gangsta rappers are black. But the fact that more than 70 percent of people who purchase gangsta rap videos are white means that it's the latter's tastes which have substantially determined the lyrics and onstage posturing of the gangsta rappers themselves. The claim by Don Imus and his supporters that his racist misogyny was simply an ill-advised attempt to mimic the language of gangsta rappers revealed that some whites use the antics of the gangsta rappers to avoid responsibility for their own deliberate unseemly behavior.

By contrast, while the achievements of individual blacks are praised, sometimes effusively, no generalizations are drawn to encompass black Americans as a whole. There's abundant praise for the athletic prowess of tennis stars Venus and Serena Williams, whose parents trained them on the public courts in Compton, California, and guided them to the pinnacle of championship tennis. But few have generalized that their success represents Black America's powerful impulse and determination to achieve. In early 2007, Wesley Autrey, a black working man and family man, caught the nation's eye for an extraordinarily heroic deed—risking his life, he saved a young man in distress from certain death under a New York City subway car. The ensuing praise, including a guest-of-honor seat at the president's State of the Union Address, was voluminous. But few suggested that Wesley Autrey's astonishing bravery and good humor represented the character of millions of other ordinary black working men and women.

Similarly, for all that's been made of the educational attainments of Barack and Michelle Obama, alumni of Ivy League colleges and Harvard Law School, there's been almost no acknowledgment that they, like many other blacks, were beneficiaries of the affirmative-action policies that opened the doors of white higher education and corporations across the land to blacks and other people of color. America as a whole continues to reap the enormous benefits that affirmative action has afforded people of color, while pretending that the policies are neither necessary nor just.

The candidacy of Barack Obama for the Democratic presidential nomination didn't cause the latest eruption of the debate over black identity. However, his being a black political path-breaker managed to underscore that the debate is more fractured than ever because the varieties of black identity are more numerous than ever. Black political path-breakers inevitably raise issues of identity because they join the idea of political representation with the symbolism of racial representation. Their very accomplishments, by differing in significant ways from how racial progress was achieved in the past, challenge the conventions of black racial identity and may provoke blacks and others to change their perceptions—and stereotypes—of blacks as a whole. They not only point to new ways that black Americans can gain high political offices once thought to be off-limits to them, but their achievements, like those of middle-class blacks in the private sector, also suggest that there are new ways of being black and American. That positive development has made some blacks anxious about new definitions of what it means to be a black American—with unfortunate consequences. That accomplished middle-class blacks like Stanley Crouch and Debra J. Dickerson would reject Barack Obama as a "real" black American because none of his black ancestors experienced slavery and because he did not have a "real" black upbringing bears witness to the numerous new fissures that have developed among blacks in America—and augurs that there will be more to come. Given blacks' firm allegiance to the Democratic Party (and the GOP's continued rejection of blacks), this fracturing of black identity won't change Black America's voting practices. But it may represent the fracturing of the high level of unanimity that's always existed within Black America on the causes of the problems besetting the black poor and how to solve them. Black America's identity—and its political success—have been built on that remarkable unanimity, on the fight of all for the triumph of inclusion over exclusion. If a substantial number of black Americans are going to begin believing they have little or nothing in common with other black Americans on the basis of class, family background, or a previous condition of servitude or not, there will be very little unanimity left in Black America.

6

TELLING THE STORIES THAT HAVE NOT BEEN TOLD

Reconstructing Black Civil Society

IT IS POSSIBLE TO IMAGINE TWO QUITE DIFFERENT scenarios for Black America in the America of, say, 2025.

In one, the black middle class has expanded to even larger numbers in the intervening decade and a half. Blacks are substantially represented throughout the media, business, and political spheres. A rising tide of prosperity that built up both the net worth and the income of the black middle class enabled it to lead the way in sharply reducing the size of the black underclass. The low unemployment rate that black Americans, like their counterparts, have long enjoyed has markedly narrowed the pipeline that used to funnel large numbers of young blacks to prison. Black America has a discernible cultural and political role at the heart of the nation, this latest stage of its emancipation and growth a direct outgrowth of the triumphs of the past in which Black America has surmounted the barriers of prejudice and disadvantage in pursuit of that most American dream: liberty and prosperity for all. And all this unfolds beneath the benign and inspiring example of the first black president of America, whoever he or she may be.

The alternative scenario is bleak. Black America has dissolved as a political force: it is still shunned by the Republican Party and increasingly ignored by the Democrats. Black political leaders, unable to coax substantive support from the mainstream political arena, have come largely to be seen as irrelevant by blacks and nonblacks alike. The great civil rights movement and the dream it set forward is increasingly viewed as a quaint moment in history. All agree that the vision of a Promised Land proved to be a mirage. The middle class, desperately trying to protect its place in an American economy battered by the forces of a globalized economy, has abandoned any effort to solve the apparently intractable problems of the black poor, who have been effectively disenfranchised. The Latino vote has grown and displaced Black America as a more coherent political force. Substantial numbers of young black men and women, whose lack of education and poor job skills have left them adrift in society, are ever more likely to be caught in a vicious cycle of imprisonment, release, joblessness, reinvolvement in crime, and reimprisonment. The black middle class has taken a beating in a national recession and sees its assets sink to a twenty-year low. The great story of Black America has ended in a corrosive rancor and divisiveness.

Stories have chapters as well as beginnings and endings. The story of Black America is at a very specific and dramatic chapter, a moment when a series of events seem to indicate that the saga's ultimate conclusion, though yet unclear, is hanging in the balance. There is a sense that while we understand what has happened, we can no longer be sure of the larger pattern into which it fits. The certainties of the purpose behind the civil rights struggle have segued into fierce debates over the morality and utility of proposed solutions to the problems black Americans continue to confront in an era when those problems stand alongside numerous examples of stunning progress.

The multicity demonstrations protesting the Jena Six case in the fall of 2007 sharply illustrated the continued use of time-honored tactics in today's different racial climate, even as it vividly displayed several of Black America's strengths: its sense of solidarity, regardless of what White America thinks; its keen sense of outrage at racial injustice; and, perhaps most of all, the ability and willingness of the mass of black Americans to organize and act on their own initiative. That display was largely ignored by the mainstream media and much of the blogosphere. Instead, their coverage of and comment on the massive, one-day demonstration in Jena and its aftermath focused on the facts and contentions of the case itself and on the involvement of the Reverends Al Sharpton and Jesse Jackson. That the protests had sprung from a grassroots, ad hoc coalition of black radio talk show hosts and disc jockeys and students from historically black colleges and universities was barely mentioned, let alone plumbed for meaning.

The significance of the Jena case, however, illuminates the predicament—and the possibilities—of the current state of Black America. Jena was only the latest high-visibility event to illustrate Black America's strengths and weaknesses, and in doing so, to clearly point toward what Black America must do if it is to save itself.

Black America's response to the Jena Six case indicates that huge numbers of black Americans—middle class, blue-collar, and poor—stand ready for mass mobilization as part of a concerted effort to attack the internal and external problems besetting them. In fact, their readiness for such an effort—a modern-day mass movement, operationally different from but rooted in the spirit of the civil rights movement—has been evident for more than a decade. That same drive was apparent in 1995 in the Million Man March, which brought more than a million black men, women, and children to the Mall in Washington, pledging to become more involved in the civic life of their communities. For months before it occurred, the march was the subject of pointed criticism from whites and blacks, primarily because its principal nominal organizer was Louis Farrakhan, the controversial, racially polarizing leader of the Nation of Islam. In addition, the march's organizers emphasized that its primary purpose was to bring black men together to focus on renewing their sense of personal integrity and their responsibilities as heads of their families and members of their communities. (The Promise Keepers, a predominantly white group with the same patriarchal focus, was also active during these years.) The organizers' seeming rejection of the participation by and even presence of women at the march and their emphasis on a patriarchal view of family duties drew sharp criticism from several prominent black women.

After the march, however, the controversy about Farrakhan's involvement and its focus on men both faded in the wake of several findings, which belied the premarch assertions of some that it would be a validation of Farrakhan's influence among blacks or an expression of black male chauvinism. Two formal studies analyzing the size of the crowd, one commissioned by the ABC network and the other by the Washington city government, found that the march had indeed lived up to its name: estimates ranged from a low of 870,000 to a high of 1.4 million; and live television coverage and newspaper articles made it clear that the throng included many black women, entire families, and even some whites.[1] Preliminary findings from a survey of more than 1,000 men at the march conducted by researchers from Howard University and a private market research group found that they were disproportionately better educated and with greater earnings than the black male population as a whole. More than a third said they had earned at least a college degree, compared to 13 percent of the general population of black males, and 41 percent of them said they earned incomes of $50,000 or more.[2]

Farrakhan's two-hour speech, which concluded the day-long event, concentrated not on racial pyrotechnics but the need for individual and communal spiritual renewal. The media coverage showed unmistakably that participants in the march were drawn by that motivation and the determination to make their presence felt. "We've been ignored," a forty-nine-year-old consumer health-care scientist and father of two daughters told a reporter who interviewed him after the march. The man, a native Alabaman, said he had marched in civil rights demonstrations in the 1960s and had tried to live King's dream, but in the decades since had often felt alone and foolish for doing so. He said his dismay changed to inspiration after a few hours at the rally. "I was in total awe of what I saw. These were men, predominantly my age, who believed the way I believed, that we should do for ourselves." Another participant, a midlevel university administrator, promised to expand the rites-of-passage program for young men he had begun several years earlier. He said, "I want to do more, for more."[3] Articles that appeared in the days, weeks, and months after the march proved that many of these men were as good as their word; they found leaders of local black organizations who said volunteerism among men had increased noticeably, particularly in such work as mentoring young boys and helping young men acquire viable job skills.[4]

That such a huge throng had assembled in the nation's capital at the site of the two most historic mass events in Black America's history—the 1963 civil rights March on Washington and the 1968 Poor People's March—made it plain that many blacks believed, three decades after legalized racism had been defeated, that something was still amiss in America and with Black America's standing in the nation as a whole. Two years later, the Million Women's March drew at least 500,000 and perhaps as many as 1 million participants to Philadelphia, another city whose history looms large for Black America. While garnering far less media coverage, this march also focused on black individuals—women—taking responsibility for their own spiritual and physical well-being and their responsibility to help strengthen black communal life.

That same quality of mobilization and mission provided an additional, powerful motivation for blacks' contributions to the post-Hurricane Katrina relief efforts. Not only were blacks far more likely than whites to have relatives or friends in the Gulf region, it quickly became apparent that blacks as a group were left most bereft by the storm. Black Americans contributed millions of dollars through such donor agencies as the American Red Cross and through national black organizations such as the National Urban League and the NAACP. Many, according to experts familiar with black philanthropic activities, also organized or took part in what amounted to a massive ad hoc relief effort carried out through churches, local community organizations, civic associations, black fraternities and sororities, and extended family networks that funneled food, clothing, furniture, cash, and gift cards for use at appliance, clothing, and home-furnishing stores in the region. Volunteers came to the stricken region ready to work one-to-two-week shifts. White Americans also organized relief efforts, but black Americans' efforts were likely more extensive because of their direct contacts with families and organizations in the areas hardest hit by the storm. Rev. John Vaughn, program officer for the Twenty-First Century Fund, a Harlem, New York-based foundation that focuses on development work in black communities, said that, although data on the extent of such ad hoc efforts hasn't been formally collected, "All indications are that these relief efforts were very widespread among blacks. Everyone has stories to tell of what their church or neighborhood group or family did on their own." Vaughn said that the local chapters and affiliates of the NAACP and National Urban League throughout the country were also "very effective" in directing emergency relief contributions to particular communities, organizations, and churches in the Gulf.[5]

In all of these events, one found, as the writer Erin Aubrey Kaplan noted of the Jena demonstration, "so very many different black people—doctors, lawyers, rappers,

Black Nationalist types—who had gathered from many points around the country for a single purpose."[6]

Kaplan caught the spirit common to these mass responses—a sense among blacks that mass mobilization was called for and an undeniable willingness to answer such a call. Since the late 1970s, the conventional wisdom has been that America has been in a post-civil-rights era, one in which the legal rights of blacks are secure and racial animus has been banished to the fringes of the society. But large majorities of black Americans have shown time and time again that they don't believe their rights are secure. The most dramatic evidence of this came in blacks' response to the 2000 presidential election vote in Florida, in which some thousands of ballots cast by blacks went uncounted and a substantial number of black voters were in various ways prevented from voting. The fact that blacks were effectively denied the right to vote—the fundamental goal of the civil rights movement—in a sharply contested election in a southern state whose suspect election total put a Republican in the White House immediately intensified blacks' distrust of the GOP and the incoming Bush administration. Their distrust was proved fully justified when, once in office, the Bush administration used its political appointees in the Justice Department to push a bogus "voter fraud" enforcement campaign designed to cull the number of black and Hispanic voters in particular districts across the country. Beyond this one glaring example, blacks have repeatedly shown in survey after survey that they believe discrimination is a commonplace fact of life for them, affecting their opportunities in the work-place, in getting admitted to college, in being treated fairly by the police and the courts, and even in being served in restaurants and department stores.

Those attitudes inform the surprising finding by the Pew Research Center, based on a survey conducted in the fall of 2007, that 60 percent of black Americans be-lieve the civil rights movement still has a "major impact" on American society. This figure represents an increase of 3 percentage points since Pew last asked the question in 1993. By contrast, the percent of whites who felt the movement still has a major impact dropped sharply during that time frame, from 66 percent to 53 percent. Interest-ingly, the survey's deeper results contradict the claim often made by conservatives that black adults who reached their maturity after the 1960s feel the movement has little rele-vance today. Pew found that 64 percent of black adults under fifty years of age—and 67 percent of those under thirty—believe the civil rights movement remains a major force in American society; only 52 percent of blacks over fifty believe that.[7]

At first glance, one might read the survey as evidence that more and more blacks believe the civil rights move-ment of the 1960s has continued to reduce the negative impact of racism on black advancement. Such a reading doesn't hold up, however. For one thing, it would make the sharp drop in white attitudes about the movement's con-tinuing relevance illogical. Furthermore, blacks' responses to other questions in the same survey show that their optimism about Black America's status has waned markedly. Just 20 percent of black Americans believe they are better off now than five years ago, 49 percent believe blacks' status is the same, and nearly a third—29 percent—believe blacks' situation has gotten worse.[8] In addition, less than half—44 percent—expect blacks' overall situation to improve in the future, a significant decline from the 57 percent who responded positively to the same question in 1986. More than one in five—21 percent—believe that blacks' situation will worsen in the future. In other words, an increasing number of black Americans are worried about blacks' progress in the present and future, and they are looking back to the civil rights movement to help them plot a way forward.

They're right to do so—not to mindlessly mimic the tactics of the past, nor to become ensnared in an endless and increasingly hollow celebration of past victories, but to understand and adapt the most important component of the twentieth-century black freedom struggle: the black American narrative.

If, when speaking about a people or an ethnic group, a narrative is the coherent arrangement of facts and myths explaining the group's past and present and embodying their hopes for the future, then Black America's modern narrative began to emerge at the turn of the twentieth century amid the legal, political, economic, and, as W. E. B. Du Bois understood, psychological devastation wrought by the *Plessy* decision. The Supreme Court had approved the reconstruction of the white supremacy narrative and its reinsertion into the political lifeblood of America. Abraham Lincoln had declared nearly a half century earlier that the American government "cannot endure permanently half slave and half free." *Plessy* was proof that White America, having eliminated Negro slavery, believed it could endure with a profoundly degraded class of those descended from slaves. Black America, constructing its narrative as it slowly built its civil society over the next half century, would, during that century's major struggle between the American traditions of inclusion and exclusion, defeat racism yet again.

It did so by using the black American narrative as a double-edged sword. It did not just tell itself—and White America—the stories that named black Americans and placed them in American history—a history they had been routinely excised from or included in as a faceless mass. It did not just tell the stories of black achievement to show that blacks belonged in the modern world, too. Nor did it, through the black newspapers that circulated widely in Black America from the turn of the century until the 1960s, merely keep count of the injustices blacks endured in the South and the North, stoking the determination to right wrongs. Blacks used the black American narrative to remind white Americans of the *ideal* American narrative, of the great humanitarian concepts on which the nation was founded and the self-evident truths the Constitution articulated. It helped immensely that, during that period, America had to fight two world wars that required it not only to rhetorically commit itself to the expansion of liberty but also to use every modern tool of communication to spread that message as widely as possible. Black Americans understood the power these words and concepts had given them: it reinforced the fact that America, "ahead of every other country in the whole Western world, large or small, has a living system of expressed ideals for human co-operation which is unified, stable, and clearly formulated."[9] The black American narrative challenged white Americans to live up to that clearly formulated system.

By the mid-1960s, that challenge so filled the American landscape and was sounded by so many different voices on both sides of the color line that it's easy to lose sight of the fact that the black American narrative had two primary stewards. One was the national black civil rights leadership that included Martin Luther King Jr., Roy Wilkins of the NAACP, Whitney M. Young Jr. of the Urban League, and Dorothy I. Height of the National Council of Negro Women. The other was the black newspapers and, pre-dominantly, the stable of magazines published by John H. Johnson—*Ebony, Jet,* and *Negro Digest.* Because the injustice was stark and pervasive, and the contrast between good and evil was clear, the black American narrative could be just as simply told. For black Americans, all of its pieces fit—even Malcolm X. His rhetorical scourging of whites acted, empathetically, to release the sometimes wracking psychological tension produced by blacks' required commitment to nonviolence, whether one was a member of the movement or not.

That history forces the obvious questions: What is the black American narrative today? What is the black American narrative's coherent explanation for affirmative action? For the increasing residential segregation of the black poor such that the problems afflicting them spin in an ever tightening circle? For Barack Obama and Condoleezza Rice? For the fact that black Americans' economic fortunes rose during the 1990s and fell during the 2001 recession—just as their white counterparts' did, but unlike whites, blacks have not recouped their economic gains? Explanations exist, of course, and have been put forth forcefully by many writers and scholars. And yet, in this age of continual, mass instantaneous access to information, Black America seems to lack a powerful, coherent narrative, one that explains Black America's present and embodies its hopes for the future, inspires black Americans and their allies, and vigorously challenges any attempt to exclude blacks from the full measure of their American citizenship.

The black American narrative lies, not in tatters but in pieces, like a shelved, unfinished manuscript because its primary guardians let go of their stewardship and their responsibility as leaders.

The Pew Research survey in November 2007 that explored black attitudes about the current state of Black America indicates that black Americans clearly sense this failure of leadership. The survey looked at three of the most important groups of the black leadership class: black politicians, the NAACP, and black ministers. This was done to align the survey question with that asked in a 1986 survey conducted by the Joint Center for Political and Economic Studies and the Gallup Poll. Those surveyed were asked to rate each group as "very effective," "somewhat effective," "not very effective," or to answer that they did not know enough about their work. The Pew survey found that when the first two rating categories were combined, all three groups scored well: 73 to 78 percent of responders rated them very or somewhat effective. But those overall figures masked sharp decreases in the "very effective" rating. Black political leaders fell from a 27 percent rating for "very effective" in 1986 to an 18 percent rating in 2007. The NAACP's drop for that category was even steeper. It fell 15 points, from a 47 percent "very effective" rating in 1986 to a 32 percent rating. The Pew survey noted that there is "strikingly, little, or no difference in these judgments . . . between those old enough to remember a time when black political leaders and the NAACP were in the forefronts of the civil rights struggles of the 1960s and '70s and later generations."[10]

Part of the reason for the falling confidence in the traditional black leadership could be gleaned from one scholar who was a longtime supporter of the traditional civil rights leadership. In the wake of the Jena Six case, he said: "I just hope it's not one of those 'situation-specific civil rights activism events'—events that fade all too soon in meaning and élan and thus never achieve an institutionalizing capability and dynamic. The post-civil-rights-movement era has . . . seen too many of such 'situation-specific civil rights activism events.'"[11] Unfortunately, that is precisely what the Jena demonstration quickly seemed to become—a "situation-specific civil rights activism event," which, like the preceding Million Man March and the Million Woman March, was destined to "fade all too soon in meaning and élan and thus never achieve an institutionalizing capability and dynamic."

This is by no means meant to suggest that the Jena demonstrations would have no effect. Just as happened after the Million Man March and, one suspects, after the Million Woman March, they very likely aided local organizations' efforts to mobilize people in black communities across the country around particular issues, and they moved individuals to become more involved in civic affairs. But none of these large-scale events, brimming with the ready-to-be-mobilized energy of hundreds of thousands of blacks, was followed by a concerted national effort to institutionalize that energy. That is, there was no systematic effort to enlist the events' participants in a range of endeavors that would produce broader, ongoing advances for Black America. For most of the twentieth century, it was the bread-and-butter work of the NAACP and the Urban League to make immediate use of incidents, events, and circumstances to organize the black masses for political action, enlist aid from the private sector, and press local, state, and federal governments for specific laws and policies. It was how they guided Black America in building a formidable institutional framework for the championing of black advancement.

This is not to say the black national leadership groups should have originated or stage-managed any of these events. In fact, it was better that the initial impetus came from outside the national black leadership structure. That grassroots action confirmed that Black America has a large segment of its population ready and eager to be mobilized to address its problems. But once the events' importance became apparent, the national black leadership should have moved quickly to capture and exploit the passion that produced them and the energy they expressed. For, singly and together, they represented the eagerness of a cross section of black Americans to address the critical, interrelated problems bedeviling the black poor: the social disarray within poor black communities that contributes to high rates of academic and disciplinary problems and other negative behavior, high rates of crime and incarceration, and, in turn, high rates of broken families trapped in a cycle of poverty. There already exist many black and predominantly black function-specific groups—some local community organizations, others white-collar professional associations—that, by focusing on a single, specific activity, have successfully sought to mitigate some of these problems.

What Black America lacks, however, is the very service it used to look chiefly to the National Urban League and the NAACP to provide: a national coordinating dynamic, and, to put it more plainly, a national sense of direction. Together, they have hundreds of chapters and affiliates. Only they have the institutional infrastructure and reach into innumerable black communities that could have quickly and reliably provided an organized means for participants in the Jena demonstrations, for example, to channel their energies into reforming the criminal justice system in their home communities. Only they have the institutional network that would enable Black America as a whole to mount a concerted national campaign to stimulate a sizable advance in black voluntary activity connecting white- and blue-collar black Americans to efforts to improve the condition of the black poor.

That kind of activity was, in its early years, also the province of the Congressional Black Caucus. But it's long past the time to stop considering the forty-three-member body a social-service agency or civil rights organization, as are the Urban League and the NAACP. The caucus must be seen as a bloc of elected politicians who constitute roughly 10 percent of the members of the House of Representatives and 1 percent (Barack Obama) of the members of the U.S. Senate. They have numerous political interests in common with the large majority of black Americans because most of them come from districts that have predominantly black electorates. But in specific terms, they are not accountable to Black America as a whole. They are accountable only to the voters in their district. So it should come as no surprise that the Congressional Black Caucus doesn't always act in a unified fashion, or that some of its members sometimes take positions or support legislation at odds with what others assert are in the best interests of Black America. Pragmatically speaking, the first duty of any politician, black politicians included, is to get reelected. That means that the national black civil rights leadership must see its relationship to the caucus as being both a pressure group for Black America and an ally of the caucus, offering the right mix of political support and political pressure to ensure that the caucus as a whole represents Black America's interests.

Both the NAACP and the National Urban League used to serve, in effect, as Black America's authoritative sources of information about everything from laws and government policies, to the latest scholarship on black affairs, to ground-level work in specific black communities. Some diminution in the extraordinary and exclusive capacity and reach they had was to be expected, as Black America itself became more variegated, and more and more function-specific groups arose to attack problems that used to be their exclusive province. The appearance of such groups not only drew the participation of individuals

who might once have gravitated to the Urban League and
the NAACP; they also drew the response of institutions—
and the support of institutional and individual donors—
that once would have looked to the latter organizations as
well. For example, from the 1930s to the 1970s, the Urban
League was at the forefront of efforts to integrate the
American workplace, from its blue-collar ranks in unions
and factories to midlevel positions in government and
corporate bureaucracies. Its officers testified at congressional hearings in the 1930s urging that blacks have equal
access to New Deal efforts to get Americans back to work,
and they lobbied the government and industry during
World War II to ensure that black workers were hired
in defense-industry plants. And they lobbied American
businesses directly, establishing seminars and training programs that brought white corporate executives to historically black colleges to discuss business issues and recruit
new employees and persuading unions in the North to establish training programs to help blacks get union cards.[12]
The Real Pepsi Challenge, which tells the story of Pepsi-
Cola's hiring in the 1940s of a special team of black advertising men and salesmen to pitch the product in black
communities, the better to compete with archrival Coca-
Cola, offers a vivid portrait of how rare it was to have black
workers at any level above janitor in white companies—and
of how difficult it was to integrate them. The story also personifies the central role the Urban League played in the
decades-long campaign. Edward F. Boyd, who led the sales

and advertising team in the late 1940s, was hired by Pepsi's president directly from his job as a special-projects officer for the Urban League.[13]

By the late 1970s, however, there were numerous other avenues blacks could use to gain access to the unions, such as government-funded training programs offered by local black organizations and the job-training programs in unions themselves that were mandated by the Nixon administration to include more black trainees. Further, corporations interested in recruiting blacks for their mid- and senior-level ranks could recruit directly from historically black and predominantly white colleges and from graduate schools of business without resorting to outside mediators. Over time, that effort has become almost completely an in-house activity, aided by the formal and informal black employee organizations and networks now standard throughout American companies. This once central function of the civil rights groups—speeding the integration of American businesses—has almost completely disappeared.

But the collapse of viable leadership has been broader than in just that one area, and it has been exacerbated by the unwillingness of the national civil rights groups over the last two decades to adequately respond to the technological advances that ushered in an era of instantaneous mass access to information and develop a varied, sophisticated communications presence. That recalcitrance has significantly harmed Black America's capacity to easily share an understanding of the nature of the problems it faces—and information about possible solutions—that it once did.

The damage that failing could cause became starkly apparent in the spring of 1993 when President Clinton nominated law professor Lani Guinier as his administration's assistant attorney general for civil rights. For Black America and for the constellation of civil rights organizations, which had been waging a bitter battle against the anti-civil-rights actions of Ronald Reagan and George H. W. Bush, Guinier was a perfect choice. She had been chief assistant in the Justice Department's Civil Rights Division during the Carter administration, and had been a top litigator at the legendary NAACP Legal Defense Fund Inc. during the 1980s before joining the law faculty at the University of Pennsylvania. In addition, after college at Radcliffe and law school at Yale—where she was a friend to Bill and Hillary Clinton—she had clerked for Damon J. Keith, a widely respected federal judge in Detroit, Michigan.

Instead, according to political science scholar Dianne M. Pinderhughes, Guinier's nomination provoked a furious attack from the right that "revealed for the first time the depth and breadth of the conservative sector's reshaped challenge to the civil rights community—and the previously unrealized weaknesses of the civil rights and voting rights lobby."[14] The civil rights groups had deferred to administration officials' request that they keep in the back-

ground and let the nomination proceed quietly because
they expected that it would, given Guinier's impeccable
educational credentials and her prior record of service in
the government and in a well-respected private public-
service agency. (Guinier herself was silent, in keeping with
White House rules that she not speak publicly until her
testimony before the Senate Judiciary Committee.) As a
result, the scope, speed, and ferocity of the attack caught
them totally unprepared. It began the day after her nomination, when one of the conservative movement's chief
"bulletin boards," the *Wall Street Journal's* op-ed page, featured a column criticizing Guinier under the headline
"Clinton's Quota Queen,"[15] and that propagandistic phrase
echoed immediately and endlessly throughout the mainstream media. Guinier's chances sunk rapidly. The civil
rights lobby never mounted an effective response to
counter the conservative control of the public debate about
Guinier. Coverage in black newspapers had been scant for
nearly a month after her nomination was announced, and
Pinderhughes noted that few editorials or op-ed pieces
supporting her appeared in white-owned newspapers until
the day after the president withdrew her nomination in
early June.

A year later, the same combination of conservative
strength in the Senate, conservative control of the media
debate, and the communications weakness of the progressive lobby forced Clinton to back away from a second
black nominee with superb credentials for the post, John

Peyton. Clinton's third nominee for the position, DeVal Patrick, the future governor of Massachusetts, was confirmed a year later. Patrick had excellent civil rights credentials, including a stint with Guinier at the NAACP Legal Defense Fund, before going into private practice. He served for three years before taking an offer to become Coca-Cola's general counsel. At that point, the conservative movement—which by then had regained control of Congress and was besieging the administration with investigations on multiple fronts—showed its strength once again by blocking Clinton's new nominee, Bill Lann Lee, an Asian American who had also been an NAACP Legal Defense Fund staff attorney. Lee, unable to clear the Republican-controlled Judiciary Committee, served as acting assistant attorney general for almost the entire remaining three years of Clinton's term.

"The point of this distressing record," Pinderhughes wrote, was that during the eight years of the Clinton presidency, "the combined force of the White House and the civil rights lobby was unable to control appointment to one of the most important administrative agencies governing voting rights policy-making litigation." A major reason for that stunning fact was that the traditional civil rights groups had been "extremely slow to respond to the sweeping revolution in information and communications technology that arrived full-bore in the 1980s and 1990s. In the early and mid-1990s, most member groups of the major civil rights lobby, the Leadership Conference on Civil Rights, passed on adopting such technological inno-

vations as e-mail and integrating them into their daily op-
erations," a stance that some continued to the end of the
decade. The choice not to join the paradigm shift in communications was to some extent understandable, given the
expense of the new technology and the need to spend
scarce resources on serving the more immediate needs of
their constituencies. An additional factor was that many
of the individuals and local community groups who comprised their grassroots constituency didn't have the new
technology, either. But it put the civil rights groups "at a
distinct disadvantage" in the competition between them
and conservative forces for quick access to and influence
over the members of Congress and the media.

By contrast, as Pinderhughes points out, the revolution
in communications technology "was expertly utilized by the
post–1960s generation of well-funded conservative organizations that had been founded to undermine the impact of
the civil rights movement victories" by defining "rights" as
something only individuals, not groups, possessed. Long
before the Guinier nomination, the conservative movement
had created its own lexicon and definitions—including
such words and phrases as "reverse discrimination" and
"quotas"—to cast the goals of the progressive organizations
in negative terms. The battle over the Clinton administration nominees to the Justice Department civil rights post
was an unmistakable demonstration of the success of the
conservative movement's long-term communications strategy. Creating their own communications outlets and network of media columnists, and cultivating reporters and

editors of the mainstream media "enabled them to seed the ground," according to Pinderhughes, "by constantly being quoted in new stories about civil rights issues and controversies and writing media columns which criticized progressive civil rights policies and pushed their own view of what constituted 'rights.' Their easy access to the mainstream media enabled them to frame the debate on a range of civil rights issues far more powerfully than had previously been the case."[16]

The defeat of the civil rights lobby was all the more dismaying because the conservative communications strategy was largely an updated version of the communications strategy that the black civil rights organizations had used from the 1900s to the 1960s to destroy legalized racism. Black America had forgotten the lessons of the playbook they had invented and employed to such great effect: a communications infrastructure of your own, utilizing numerous voices to emphasize one message, is vital to educating the public and inspiring it to help you shape the debate and influence the media and, ultimately, the decision-makers in government and the private sector.

Unfortunately, little has changed in that regard, as shown by the weak public presence of the Urban League and the NAACP in the debates over Bush's nominations of John Roberts and Samuel Alito to the U.S. Supreme Court. Theoretically, both the NAACP and the Urban League could have launched a communications blitz against the nominations: both had general-interest magazines aimed at Black America. But neither was ready for

such an effort. Inexplicably, the Urban League was virtually AWOL from the debate over both nominations. The
NAACP and the rest of the civil rights coalition lobbied
vigorously against Roberts and Alito, but one had to be
inside the Beltway or inside the civil rights loop to know
it. Very little of their work or positions was written about
or aired in the mainstream media, and the limited reach
of black newspapers meant that much of Black America
was left uninformed about why it was important to oppose the two nominees.

Indeed, the NAACP and the Urban League must share
a large measure of the blame for Black America's declining confidence in the national black leadership because
during the Jim Crow decades, they were the primary stewards of the black American narrative. Their own historic
publications—*The Crisis,* which the NAACP founded in
1910, and *Opportunity Journal,* which the Urban League
founded in 1923—had played crucial roles in constructing
that narrative. In addition, during the 1970s and 1980s,
the Urban League's annual public-policy report, *The State
of Black America,* was widely considered an important
source for statistical information and perspective from
scholars and public-policy experts on the problems facing
black Americans. These publications' pioneering work in
using dispassionate scholarship, journalism, and the tech-
niques of propaganda to educate the public and advance
their public-policy interests makes the organizations' abandonment of that legacy in the era of mass instantaneous
communication all the more startling. During the past

quarter century—while the universe of conservative foundations and think tanks developed a wide array of print
magazines and wonkish journals, Webzines, and rapid-
response blogs that effectively influenced mainstream media coverage, public opinion, and political action on a wide
range of issues—Black America's two leading national
groups have been content to have their publications, both
revived in the late 1990s, appear just a few times a year, and
they have developed no rapid-response Internet capability
at all.

For nearly a decade, *The Crisis* appeared six times a year;
Opportunity Journal's frequency of publication was far
more sporadic, never appearing more than four times a
year and sometimes appearing only once. As editor of
both *Opportunity Journal* and *The State of Black America* for
nearly ten years before leaving the Urban League in 2005,
I wrote numerous memos describing both the need for
and financial viability of increasing the *Opportunity Journal* to a monthly magazine and changing *The State of Black
America* to a twice-a-year publication and establishing an
online weekly that would respond to current events. As
with the NAACP, the Urban League's publications were
protected from the exacting financial rigors of the market-
place by its nonprofit status. The publications needed only
to break even. But I also believed that they could become
profitable through the advertising revenues they would
draw from companies that would see the Urban League,
which had the reputation as a thoroughly middle-class or-

ganization, as another venue to offer their products to the growing black middle class. My suggestions were ignored. Indeed, during my last years there, Marc Morial, the president of the Urban League, rather than provide additional financial support to *Opportunity Journal* and *The State of Black America*, established a new publication, *Urban Influence*, that he described as a "lifestyle magazine," managed completely by outside consultants. When I asked him why the National Urban League, a public-policy organization, would want to publish a magazine devoted to lifestyle pursuits, he said its purpose was to attract young adults to the league. *Urban Influence* regularly appeared six times a year, but its actual circulation was never made clear. During those same years, *Opportunity Journal* never appeared more than three times a year. Meanwhile, with the disappearance in 2000 of *Emerge,* the tough-minded, provocative general-interest magazine, Black America was left with no widely circulating publication that covered current events that blacks were most interested in. (In mid-2007, the NAACP hired a new editor for *The Crisis,* hopefully indicating its determination to build it back into an important publication.)

The story of the self-imposed decline of the Urban League and NAACP publications is important because in this period, during which the twenty-four-hour news cycle and instant mass access to the channels of communication emerged, the organizations and Black America as a whole were left largely dependent on the mainstream media to get their message out to a broad public and to participate in the public discourse. That, in turn, meant that they had lost the ability to maintain, and refresh, the black American narrative: to quickly communicate with their core constituency about their programs and activities and to recruit new supporters; to quickly interpret new developments within and outside of Black America in ways that would establish those developments' relationship to the continuing group narrative; and to effectively contest views that harm the interests of Black America. Many of the local chapters and affiliates of the two organizations remain effective advocates in their communities. But at the national level, the views of the NAACP and the Urban League on pressing public-policy issues, be it the economy, education, sentencing reform, or health care, have long since disappeared from the mainstream media—from which blacks overwhelmingly get their news—and from the general discourse. In that regard, they have become largely invisible.

The effectiveness of black radio disc jockeys and Internet-savvy black college students in stimulating the massive black response to the Jena Six case was an implicit rebuke to the failure of the national black leadership to properly manage its relationship with its core constituency. So, too, was the stunning success in 2006 of *The Covenant with Black America*, the book edited by talk show host Tavis Smiley. The paperback contained brief essays outlining ten problems confronting blacks (health care, crime and the criminal justice system, public schools, etc.) and listing specific ways to attack these problems. For each problem, the author described successful efforts by several local organizations in different parts of the country to address it. Fueled by Smiley's grassroots promotion effort, the book shot to the top of the *New York Times* best-selling paperback list, where it remained for several weeks. Its success was a striking snapshot of the hunger within Black America for a discussion about how to solve the problems plaguing their communities. That hunger had long been obvious, but through the late 1990s and first years of the new century, the Urban League and NAACP became increasingly indifferent to it. Smiley produced a second "how-to" book, *The Covenant in Action,* which was, in effect, a more populist version of the Urban League's *The State of Black America.* Its articles were matter-of-fact, not scholarly in tone, and they got right to the point: This is what's wrong. These are some ways to fix it. These are some organizations that are making a difference. There is no reason the two books couldn't coexist. Certainly, given the growing number of black (and non-black) scholars in academia, public-policy wonks in think tanks and foundations, and on legislative staffs for local, state, and federal governments, and working as journalists and community activists, there is no shortage of talent to fill the pages of these and several more serious news publications aimed at Black America. But in the wake of *The Covenant, The State of Black America* has become less, not more, visible.

It's difficult to understand this dereliction of duty except as part of an overall lost sense of mission by the organizations' leadership. There is, of course, plenty of evidence that such a falling-off of organizational leader-ship is hardly exclusive to black institutions. The last de-cade in America is replete with startling examples of the decline of white leadership—including the decline of Congress as a deliberative body, the multiple ethical scan-dals that led to the virtual collapse of the Bush adminis-tration and the Republican Party, and the crony-capitalist scandals that for a time transformed newspaper business pages into crime sheets.

That said, the loss of institutional vision and discipline at the top of the NAACP and Urban League hurts Black America more in comparative terms because its overall resources are so relatively meager and the problems af-flicting its sizable group of poor people are so great.

Can the National Urban League and the NAACP re-gain their effectiveness as national organizations? Can they regain the confidence that Black America is losing in them? Only if they give themselves over to what must become their two primary responsibilities. One is to estab-lish a modern, multidimensional communications appa-ratus so that they can reestablish a connection with the masses of black Americans, bring the masses of black Americans more directly into the discussion of ideas about and policy for the future of America, and thereby perpetu-ate the black American narrative. Second, these organi-zations' national leadership must devote themselves more directly and more vigorously to helping the black poor, both by developing more programs targeting the black

poor that are national in scope and by becoming a clear-
inghouse of information on local programs across the
country that aid the black poor. In fact, local NAACP
chapters and Urban League affiliates routinely serve as
clearinghouses of information in their own communities,
and the Urban League's once-widely respected research
unit used to perform that role at the national level. It desperately needs to be revived. Doing so would help them
stoke and channel the problem-solving energies of blacks
into constructive activities at the local, state, and national
levels, and provide tangible proof that these organizations,
both of which are approaching their centennial anniversaries, still have vital roles to play in forging Black America's present and future.

The declining vigor of the major national black civil rights
groups adds another threat to the future viability of Black
America. Its fortunes have risen and its marked advances
have been achieved in times of widespread prosperity, such
as the 1990s, when the country's economic bounty expands
opportunity in numerous sectors of the social landscape.
But that kind of era is not on the economic horizon. The
sinking prospects of the U.S. economy and the collapse of
the subprime mortgage market will continue to put great
financial pressure not only on the black poor but also on
many blacks in the middle class. Indeed, the radiating impact of the housing crisis is likely to push a significant

number of middle- and lower-middle-class blacks several rungs down the income ladder. The jobless recovery prevented black Americans from recouping their financial gains of the 1990s after the 2001 recession had wiped them out. If the economy continues to sour, black Americans' economic pain will be widespread, and the economic pain throughout America will deepen, limiting the resources and very likely depressing the societal will to address Black America's critical social problems. The astronomic costs of the U.S. involvement in Iraq will continue to drain billions of dollars from the nation's economy that could have been put to domestic use stimulating job creation and supporting broadscale social needs. In addition, America's need to respond to the Latino immigration crisis, disrupted in 2007 by the fierce backlash the conservative rank and file launched against the ill-fated compromise legislation in Congress, is certain to explode again, raising the prospect of a society-wide polarization not seen since the late 1960s. Such a development would further diminish the willingness of the public at large to demand that Congress address many of the urgent issues affecting the poor in general and the black poor in particular.

That gloomy prospect underscores that, for black Americans, a Democratic administration in the White House and Democratic control of Congress is essential. It is their only chance not to eliminate but to narrow the scope of the difficulties that lie ahead. For blacks, the Republican Party continues to be the party of no choice. It is a measure of both the party's hostility to blacks and the persistence of the dynamic of racial exclusion that after a quarter century of holding substantial political office and power, the GOP has no elected black representative or senator in Congress, no black official in the high command of the party structure, and fewer than fifty black Republicans holding political office of any kind in the entire country. Moreover, they have fielded a cast vying for the Republican presidential nomination who, with few exceptions, went out of their way to insult black voters in order to appeal to their conservative base. Despite the considerable good that blacks have forged from their involvement in the Democratic Party, their political segregation continues to retard their full assimilation into American society.

Nonetheless, there is considerable cause for believing that black Americans have a fighting chance to wage the struggle for their future if only because they have had as a foil an administration whose unparalleled incompetence and callousness has been to the shame of America in general, and it seems likely to stand as a benchmark in political recidivism. To have been ignored by that kind of GOP is perversely inspiring, even if it is at odds with the progressive exercise of real political power and influence. The 2006 midterm results do not guarantee that Black America will secure the legislation and government policies needed to help alleviate the social problems of the black poor and counter the seemingly race-neutral policies and practices that are a continuing barrier to black progress. But they do expand the room and opportunity that blacks have to play politics at the center of American society. The 2006 election catapulted more than a dozen black congressional Democrats to committee and subcommittee chairmanships; put another black Democrat in a state governor's office for only the second time in more than a century; and brought forward Black America's first black mainstream candidate for a party nomination for president.

Black Americans have also been fortunate in that the contest for the Democratic presidential nomination, as expected, brought forward the first white woman who had a credible chance to win. The presence of Hillary Clinton and Barack Obama as the two front-runners enabled the mass of black Americans to simultaneously show their racial loyalty to a black politician, their loyalty to a nonblack politician they trust, and their political pragmatism in moving their support to the candidate they believed had the best chance of winning both the nomination and the ultimate prize, the White House. If either Hillary Clinton or Barack Obama is elected president, the winner will know that he or she owes the victory to a high turnout of black Americans. Either candidate, therefore, can plausibly be said to be the best for Black America.

But the importance of Clinton and Obama as political figures in their own right and as symbols of blacks' political sophistication must not be allowed to obscure the broader issue. Black America needs to have an effective and sustained voice that isn't dependent on one man or woman, or even on a single political party. Our society—at least our political society—for better or worse is a crucible where those who wield influence wield power. Power transfers from senator to lobbyist, from corporation to candidate. In this world, Black America is still a child playing out of its range. The only way for Black America to compete is for the representatives of Black America—the NAACP and the National Urban League most notably—to up their game substantially. The task ahead is to once again find the volcanic, self-starting organizing power that produced the Jena Six demonstrations and the Million Man and Woman marches and to yoke it to the ongoing mission of Black America. If there is unfinished business from the civil rights era, then it is the current generation's responsibility to finish it, and not to let it slide back. The moral example of the civil rights era and the longer struggle for black political and social representation in America is as powerful today as ever. Parts of the political electorate are fond of talking about values: Black America needs to boldly remind the country that the whole of America benefited from the vision of the civil rights era, that black American history is a continuous and ongoing part of the national fabric, and that Black America is a unique political and social force that has kept this country honest for more than a century. The future of Black America matters to every American.

ACKNOWLEDGMENTS

I HAVE ALWAYS COUNTED MYSELF FORTUNATE TO HAVE come of age during the 1960s—to have been able to bear witness to what America was as the black freedom struggle was teaching White America how to practice democracy, and to be in the first generation of black Americans who had the freedom not only to dream American dreams but to pursue them. From a comfortable perch in the North, I immersed myself in black Americans' history, and I watched and read about the heroic efforts of all those, old and young, participating in the movement. I felt an intense obligation. That realization was an inspiration, not a burden, because it was the black freedom struggle that made my future possible. This book is a product of that treasured sense of obligation, a small payment down on the immense debt I owe. It would not have come to fruition, however, without the contributions to me and the patience with me on the part of many people. I thank Walter Stafford, a committed scholar and activist, for his support of my work before I began this book and his crucial support while I was formulating the ideas that led to its creation. I am very grateful for the several conversations I had with Cheryl Woodruff that helped sharpen my thinking about the lines of inquiry I wanted to pursue and how I wanted to pursue them. Walter L. Leib provided a bracing moral support at an early stage that helped me move forward with my work. Hilary A. Lewis, a stalwart, wonderful friend whose writing has been a model for my own, tolerated my ramblings about black politics and numerous other subjects while trying her brilliant best to force me to give them intellectual coherence. I also thank Douglas E. Schoen, Charles N. Atkins, Phillip Page, Beverly Edgehill, David A. Thomas, Peter Williams, Maurice "Mickey" Carroll, Mark Chichester, Ernest J. Wilson III, Dennis C. Dickerson, Ronald W. Walters, Randolph McGlocklin, and Henry McGee for sharing their insights with me. Nancy Kurtz, David Klatell, Addie Rimmer, and June Cross, by requiring me to work on other projects in the midst of my research, helped me to focus more on this book than they know. John and Marianne Shearer, Lewis and Kristin Jones, and Charles and Suzanne Randolph Shorter, and Sharon Combs, longtime friends, held me even closer to them during this project; our conversations always brought comfort and inspiration. Through my friendship with Rose Jefferson-Frazier, I have learned how to be more disciplined and have the courage to work harder; she personifies the meaning of perseverance and resourcefulness. Vie Kaufman has been not only a valued friend and colleague, but also a guardian angel to this book from beginning to end. My gratitude to Charles J. Hamilton Jr. and Pamela Carlton Hamilton, who hovered over this project as intellectual godfather and godmother, is immense. As always, my family—Leslie Vance, Lois Tyler Dwyer and Bill Dwyer, Lloyd A. Daniels Jr. and Linda Daniels, Evelyn Tyler, Elaine Tyler and Jan Zimmerman, David Daniels, Sedi Daniels, Cecilie Vance Penchion and Mickey Penchion, and Courtney B. Vance and Angela Bassett Vance—has offered more emotional support than I could ever deserve. I didn't think it possible, but through this project, I've grown to love even more Monroe "Bud" Moseley and Frances Kenney Moseley, and to be more amazed and thankful that I've done something to deserve the support of Anne K. Kenney all these years. One of the great pleasures of working on this book is that it led to a friendship with Vernon E. Jordan Jr. Anyone who's had that privilege will agree that not only is he a great man, he is a great pal. There are no words to adequately describe Courtney Lang's contribution to this work. Her fierce, provocative intelligence, her intolerance for falsehood and posturing, and her commitment to Black America's present and future make my gratitude to her boundless. This book could not have appeared without the extraordinary faith and hard work of my agent, Sarah Lazin, and my editor, Clive Priddle. They were working with very hard clay, and their determination and conviction that my point of view had value made this book possible. Finally, I continue to be more thankful than I can ever convey for becoming, first, a student of Martin L. Kilson, and then part of the family of Martin and Marion Kilson. They have always represented a standard of intellectual achievement that I am still trying to meet.

NOTES

INTRODUCTION

1. Bret Stephens, "Barack Obama shows why foreigners consider us naïve," *Wall Street Journal,* January 8, 2008.

CHAPTER 1

1. Patrick Healy and Jeff Zelany, "Clinton and Obama Unite in Pleas to Blacks," *New York Times,* March 5, 2007.

2. Albert Hunt, "As Obama, Clinton Seek Votes, All Blacks Win," *Bloomberg.com News,* March 5, 2007.

3. Darryl Fears, "NAACP Will Cut Staffing, Close Offices," *Washington Post,* June 8, 2007.

4. Tom Wicker, "Kennedy and Our Vanished Dreams," *New York Times Magazine,* November 20, 1983, 73.

5. Jeffrey Toobin, *The Nine: Inside the Secret World of the Supreme Court* (New York: Doubleday, 2007), 213–214.

6. Ibid., 224.

7. Perry Bacon Jr., "Here Come the New Wave of Barack Obamas," *Time*, August 7, 2006, http://www.time.com/time/nation/article/0,8599,1223497,00.html.

8. Bliss Broyard, *One Drop: My Father's Hidden Life—A Story of Race and Family Secrets* (New York: Little, Brown & Co., 2007).

9. James Oliver Horton and Lois E. Horton, *Slavery and the Making of America* (Oxford: Oxford University Press, 2005), 157–58.

10. Michael K. Fauntroy, *Republicans and the Black Vote* (Boulder, CO: Lynne Rienner Publishers, 2007), 76.

CHAPTER 2

1. U.S. Census Bureau, *The American Community—Blacks: 2004*, February 2007, Table 11.

2. Economic Policy Institute, *The State of Working America 2006/2007* (June 2007), Chapter 5, Table 5.11, 266.

3. U.S. Census Bureau, *The American Community*, Tables 13, 14, 15.

4. "Black Enrollments in Higher Education Continue to Climb," *The Journal of Blacks in Higher Education*, Number 56 (Summer 2007): 30.

5. "Snail-Like Progress in Increasing Black Coaches and Administrators in College Sports," *Journal of Blacks in Higher Education*, no. 56 (Summer 2007): 40–41.

6. The Wells quotation comes from "Law Firms Are Slow in Promoting Minority Lawyers to Partnerships," *New York Times*, August 7, 2001.

7. Susan D. Toliver, *Black Families in Corporate America* (London: Sage Publications, 1998), 4–5.

8. Robert C. Lieberman, "'The Storm Didn't Discriminate': Katrina and the Politics of Color Blindness," *Du Bois Review* 3 (2006): 7–8.

9. Nelson D. Schwartz, "Can a Mortgage Crisis Swallow a Town?" *New York Times*, September 2, 2007.

NOTES   203

10. Ford Fessenden, "The American Dream Foreclosed," *New York Times*, October 14, 2007.

11. Gretchen Morgenson, "Dubious Fees Hit Borrowers in Foreclosures," *New York Times*, November 6, 2007.

12. Vikas Bajaj and Ford Fessenden, "What's Behind the Race Gap?" *New York Times*, November 4, 2007.

13. Ron Nixon, "Study Predicts Foreclosure for 1 in 5 Subprime Loans," *New York Times*, December 20, 2006.

14. Samuel L. Myers Jr., "African American Economic Well-Being During the Boom and Bust," in *The State of Black America 2004*, ed. Lee A. Daniels (New York: The National Urban League, 2004), 60.

15. Bajaj and Fessenden, "What's Behind the Race Gap?"

16. Myers Jr., "African American Economic Well-Being," Figure 3, 58.

17. Nixon, "Study Predicts Foreclosure."

18. Vokas Bajaj and Ron Nixon, "For Minorities, Signs of Trouble in Foreclosures," *New York Times*, February 22, 2006; Economic Policy Institute, *The State of Working America 2006/2007*, Chapter 5, Table 5.11, 266.

19. Christian E. Weller and Eli Staub, "Middle Class in Turmoil: Economic Risks Up Sharply for Most Families Since 2001" (Washington, D.C.: The Center for American Progress, 2007), 1–2.

20. Economic Policy Institute, *Working America*, Introduction, Table 1.6.

21. Economic Policy Institute, *Working America*, 255–257.

22. John J. Havens and Paul G. Schervish, "Wealth Transfer Estimates for African American Households," *New Directions for Philanthropic Fundraising* 48 (2005): Table 5.

23. Ibid., 19.

24. Franklin D. Raines, "What Would Equality Look Like: Reflections on the Past, Present and Future," *The State of Black America 2002*, ed. Lee A. Daniels (New York: The National Urban League, 2002), 17.

25. Joe Davidson, "Bob Johnson on Black Wealth," in *Being A Black Man: At the Corner of Progress and Peril,* eds. The Staff of the *Washington Post* (New York: PublicAffairs, 2007), 259.

26. Ken Smikle, ed., "The Buying Power of Black America 2005," *Target Market News,* 2005.

27. Myers Jr., "African American Economic Well-Being," 66.

CHAPTER 3

1. Harvey Fireside, "Homage to Homer: Remembering *Plessy v. Ferguson* and the Courage of the Man Who Defied Discrimination," *Opportunity Journal* 17 (Spring 2004): 7.

2. Nicholas Lemann, *The Promised Land: The Great Black Migration and How It Changed America* (New York: Knopf, 1991), 6.

3. See Farah Jasmine Griffin, *Who Set You Flowin'? The African-American Migration Narrative* (Oxford: Oxford University Press, 1995), for a brilliant exploration of the psychological importance of the migration dynamic to the black experience.

4. Douglas S. Massey, *Categorically Unequal: The American Stratification System* (New York: Russell Sage Foundation, 2007), 56–57.

5. Ibid., 60–62.

6. Ibid., 63–65.

7. U.S. Census Bureau, *The American Community—Blacks 2004,* American Community Survey Reports, February 2007, Figure 13.

8. Nicholas D. Kristof, "The Cheerleader: Earning A's in People Skills at Andover," *New York Times,* June 10, 2000.

9. Nicholas D. Kristof, "The Texas Governor: Ally of an Older Generation amid the Tumult of the 60's," *New York Times,* June 19, 2000.

10. Marilyn Kiss, "A Ticket to Andover," *New York Times,* June 14, 2000.

11. Daniel Golden, *The Price of Admission: How America's Ruling Class Buys Its Way Into Elite Colleges—and Who gets Left Outside the Gates* (New York: Crown, 2006), 4–6.

12. "Blacks Convinced Discrimination Still Exists in College Admissions Process," The Gallup Poll, August 24, 2007.

13. Walter W. Stafford, "The National Urban League Survey: Black America's Under–35 Generation," *The State of Black America 2001* (August 2001), Tables 10, 11, 47–48.

14. Susan D. Toliver, *Black Families in Corporate America* (London: Sage Publications, 1998), 16.

15. Ibid., 46–47.

16. Joe Davidson, "Bob Johnson on Black Wealth," in *Being A Black Man: At the Corner of Progress and Peril,* eds. The Staff of the *Washington Post* (New York: PublicAffairs, 2007), 253.

17. Martin L. Kilson, "Thinking about the Black Elite's Role: Yesterday and Today," in *The State of Black America 2005* (New York: The National Urban League, 2005), 93.

18. Ibid.; Pei-te Lien, Dianne M. Pinderhughes, Carol Hardy-Fanta, Christine M. Sierra, "The Voting Rights Act and the Election of Non-White Officials," *PS: Political Science and Politics,* July 2007, 489–494.

19. National Bureau of Economic Research, "Area Economic Conditions and the Labor Market Outcomes of Young Men in the 1990s Expansion," Working Paper 7073, April 1999.

20. Sara Rimer, "Job Opportunities Bring Out Young People (and Their Idealism) in Riot Area," *New York Times,* June 18, 1992.

CHAPTER 4

1. John M. Broder, "The 2000 Campaign: The Ad Campaign: Emotional Appeal Urges Blacks to Vote," *New York Times,* November 2, 2000.

2. Michael A. Fletcher, "GOP Plans More Outreach to Blacks, Mehlman Says," *Washington Post,* August 7, 2005.

3. Michael K. Fauntroy, *Republicans and the Black Vote* (Boulder, CO: Lynne Rienner Publishers, 2007), 5.

4. Taylor Branch, *Parting the Waters: America in the King Years, 1954–1963* (New York: Simon and Schuster, 1989), 362–366.

5. Theodore H. White, *The Making of The President, 1960* (New York: New American Library, 1961), 403–404.

6. Fauntroy, *Republicans and the Black Vote*, 51.

7. Ibid.

8. Thomas B. Edsall, *Building Red America: The New Conservative Coalition and the Drive for Permanent Power* (New York: Basic Books, 2006), 9–10.

9. Fauntroy, *Republicans and the Black Vote*, 5.

10. David Brooks, "History and Calumny," *New York Times*, November 9, 2007.

11. Lou Cannon, "Reagan's Southern Stumble," *New York Times*, November 18, 2007.

12. Thomas F. Shaller, *Whistling Past Dixie: How Democrats Can Win Without the South* (New York: Simon & Schuster, 2006), 22–23.

13. Lee A. Daniels, "The New Black Conservatives," *New York Times Magazine,* October 4, 1981, 21.

14. Fauntroy, *Republicans and the Black Vote,* 5.

15. Charles V. Hamilton, "Joining the Political Process," in *The Fairmont Papers: Black Alternatives' Conference* (San Francisco: Institute for Contemporary Studies, 1981), 122.

16. Martin Kilson, "Widening Our Reach," in *The Fairmont Papers: Black Alternatives' Conference* (San Francisco: Institute for Contemporary Studies, 1981), 134–137.

17. Daniels, "The New Black Conservatives," 23.

18. Joe Davidson, "Bob Johnson on Black Wealth," in *Being a Black Man: At the Corner of Progress and Peril,* eds. The Staff of the *Washington Post* (New York: Public Affairs, 2007), 253.

19. Gerald M. Boyd, "President Meets with 20 Blacks; Intent Disputed," *New York Times,* January 16, 1985.

20. Bernard Weinraub, "President Asserts Black Leadership Twists His Record," *New York Times,* January 19, 1985.

21. Ta-Nehisi Coates, "The Irrelevant Rev. Sharpton," *Washington Post,* October 28, 2007.

22. Juan Williams, "GOP Blacks Complain of Limited Access," *Washington Post,* January 28, 1985.

23. Fauntroy, *Republicans and the Black Vote*, 146.

24. Martin L. Kilson, "African Americans and American Politics 2002: The Maturation Phase," in *The State of Black America 2002* (New York: National Urban League, 2002), 148–149.

25. Adam Nagourney and Anne E. Kornblut, "White House Enacts a Plan to End Political Damage," *New York Times*, September 5, 2005.

26. Kevin Drum, "Bush and Katrina," *Washington Monthly*, September 6, 2005.

27. Pew Research Center for the People and the Press, "Huge Racial Divide over Katrina and its Consequences," September 8, 2005, 2, 3.

28. Dan Froomkin, "A Polling Free-Fall among Blacks," *Washington Post*, October 13, 2005.

29. Marc H. Morial, "Hurricane Katrina's Continuing Crisis— and Opportunity," *To Be Equal* 40 (2005), National Urban League, September 12, 2005, http://www.nul.org//publications/TBE/2005/TBE-COL-40.pdf.

30. Ibid.

31. Ibid.

32. Pew Research Center, "Huge Racial Divide over Katrina and its Consequences," 3.

33. Morial, "Hurricane Katrina's Continuing Crisis—and Opportunity."

34. Michael Cottman, "Black Republicans Fear Botched Katrina Response May Impact Outreach," *Washington Post*, September 28, 2005.

35. "The Best Coverage Money Can Buy," *New York Times*, http://query.nytimes.com/gst/fullpage.html?res=9401E7DF 173BF934A15752C0A9639C8B63&sec=&spon=&partner =permalink&exprod=permalink.

Chapter 5

1. Richard Wolffe and Daren Briscoe, "Following His Instincts," *Newsweek*, July 16, 2007, http://www.newsweek.com/id/33201.

2. Charles Krauthammer, "Winning By Losing," *Washington Post*, October 27, 2006.

3. Stanley Crouch, "What Obama Isn't: Black Like Me," *New York Daily News,* November 2, 2006.

4. Debra J. Dickerson, "Colorblind," *Salon,* January 22, 2007, http://www.salon.com/opinion/feature/2007/01/22/obama/index.html?source=search&aim=/opinion/feature.

5. Debra J. Dickerson, *The End of Blackness: Returning the Souls of Black Folk to Their Rightful Owners* (New York: Anchor Books, 2005), 12–13.

6. Debra J. Dickerson, "Don't Be Black on My Account," *Salon*, March 5, 2007, http://www.salon.com/opinion/feature/2007/03/05/kids/index.html?source=search&aim=/opinion/feature.

7. Dickerson, "Colorblind," *Salon.*

8. W. E. B. Du Bois, *The Souls of Black Folk* (New York: Signet Classics, 1969), 2.

9. Ibid., 14–15.

10. Henry James, *New York Revisited* (New York: Franklin Square Press, 1994), 46–47.

11. John H. Johnson, *Ebony,* August 1965, 27.

12. John Leo, "Militants Object to 'Negro' Usage," *New York Times,* February 26, 1968.

13. Associated Press, "Jackson and Others Say 'Blacks' is Passé," *New York Times*, December 21, 1988.

14. "'African-American' Favored by Many of America's Blacks," *New York Times*, January 31, 1989.

15. Howard Witt, "School Discipline Tougher on African Americans," *Chicago Tribune,* September 24, 2007.

CHAPTER 6

1. Michael Janofsky, "Federal Parks Chief Calls 'Million Man' Count Low," *New York Times,* October 21, 1995.

2. Michel Marriott, "Another Majority, Silent and Black," *New York Times*, October 22, 1995.

3. Ibid.

4. Jonathan P. Hicks, "Answering the March's Call: More Community Involvement by Black Men," *New York Times,* December 29, 1995.

5. Rev. John Vaughn, in interview with the author, August 22, 2007.

6. Erin Aubrey Kaplan, "After Jena," *Salon,* September 25, 2007, http://www.salon.com/opinion/feature/2007/09/25/jena/index.html?source=search&aim=/opinion/feature.

7. Pew Research Center for the People and the Press, "Optimism about Black Progress Declines: Blacks See Growing Values Gap Between Poor and Middle Class," Table: "Civil Rights Movement Still Important, but Less So" and Table: "Optimism About Black Progress Declines," November 13, 2007, 57.

8. Pew Research Center for the People and the Press, "Optimism about Black Progress Declines: Blacks See Growing Values Gap Between Poor and Middle Class;" "Is the Situation of Blacks Better, Worse, or the Same?" November 13, 2007, 17.

9. Gene Roberts and Hank Klibanoff, *The Race Beat: The Press, The Civil Rights Struggle, and the Awakening of a Nation* (New York: Knopf, 2006), 4; Walter A. Jackson, *Gunnar Myrdal and America's Conscience: Social Engineering and Racial Liberalism, 1938–1987* (Chapel Hill: University of North Carolina Press, 1990), 149.

10. Pew Research Center for the People and the Press, "Optimism about Black Progress Declines: Blacks See Growing Values Gap Between Poor and Middle Class," Table: "Declining Ratings of Black Leaders' Effectiveness," November 13, 2007, 56.

11. Personal communication to the author, September 22, 2007.

12. Dona Cooper Hamilton and Charles V. Hamilton, *Dual Agenda: The African-American Struggle for Civil and Economic Equality* (New York: Columbia University Press, 1997), 9–66.

13. Stephanie Capparell, *The Real Pepsi Challenge: The Inspirational Story of Breaking the Color Barrier in American Business* (New York: Wall Street Journal Books, 2007), 65.

14. Dianne Pinderhughes, "The Renewal of the Voting Rights Act," in *The State of Black America 2005* (New York: The National Urban League, 2005), 54.

15. Clint Bolick, Op-Ed, *Wall Street Journal,* April 30, 1993.

16. Pinderhughes, "The Renewal of the Voting Rights Act," 55–56.

INDEX

Lee A. Daniels was, until 2005, the editor of the
National Urban League's public policy journal
The State of Black America. For twenty years, he
was a reporter for the *New York Times* and the
Washington Post. Born in Boston, he now lives in
New York City.

PublicAffairs is a publishing house founded in 1997. It is a tribute to the standards, values, and flair of three persons who have served as mentors to countless reporters, writers, editors, and book people of all kinds, including me.

I. F. STONE, proprietor of *I. F. Stone's Weekly*, combined a commitment to the First Amendment with entrepreneurial zeal and reporting skill and became one of the great independent journalists in American history. At the age of eighty, Izzy published *The Trial of Socrates*, which was a national bestseller. He wrote the book after he taught himself ancient Greek.

BENJAMIN C. BRADLEE was for nearly thirty years the charismatic editorial leader of *The Washington Post*. It was Ben who gave the *Post* the range and courage to pursue such historic issues as Watergate. He supported his reporters with a tenacity that made them fearless and it is no accident that so many became authors of influential, best-selling books.

ROBERT L. BERNSTEIN, the chief executive of Random House for more than a quarter century, guided one of the nation's premier publishing houses. Bob was personally responsible for many books of political dissent and argument that challenged tyranny around the globe. He is also the founder and longtime chair of Human Rights Watch, one of the most respected human rights organizations in the world.

· · ·

For fifty years, the banner of Public Affairs Press was carried by its owner Morris B. Schnapper, who published Gandhi, Nasser, Toynbee, Truman, and about 1,500 other authors. In 1983, Schnapper was described by *The Washington Post* as "a redoubtable gadfly." His legacy will endure in the books to come.

Peter Osnos, *Founder and Editor-at-Large*